A Just Church

A Just Church

21st century liberation theology in action

Chris Howson

continuum

Published by the Continuum International Publishing Group

The Tower Building, 11 York Road, London SE1 7NX

80 Maiden Lane, Suite 704, New York NY 10038

www.continuumbooks.com

First published 2011

British Library Cataloguing-in-Publication Data

A catalogue record for this book is available from the British Library.

ISBN: 978–1–4411–9992–8 (paperback)

Designed and typeset by Kenneth Burnley, Wirral, Cheshire

Printed and bound in India by Replika Press Pvt Ltd

Contents

For Renu and all those who feel the pain of this life.

For Mary, CJ and Angel and all who work for 'another possible world'.

'Blessed are those who hunger and thirst for justice, for they shall be satisfied.' (Matthew 5.6)

Foreword

Bradford is rightfully considered to be a tough place in which to minister. The increase in the proportion of people of other faiths in the city inevitably has a downward impact on church attendance. Common sense would then expect that churches in Bradford endure repeated crises in relation to viability. There are indeed instances of this, but what is presented here offers a different story from that city. It is a story of passion and innovation. It shouldn't surprise us that new things are happening in Bradford. The city has an impressive tradition of innovation. It pioneered building societies and penny banks, choral societies and co-operative societies and feisty suffragettes long before other places.

Public theology is a vital tool in a city like Bradford where religion can often be intensely debated – and suspected. Public theology is concerned with the wide relevance of the gospel. It assumes that the insights from the Christian faith are relevant to everyone, not just Christians; but public theology also acknowledges that Christian insights are just one perspective within a diverse compendium of ideas. This requires an intellectual rigour but also imaginative and committed 'praxis', otherwise what is offered is reduced to 'mere rhetoric' and is judged as 'empty'.

Public theology is essentially a humble affair because of the recognition that the Christian voice is just one of the voices in the market place and can command no special hearing. Christian leaders in Bradford have embraced such humility for over two decades. It is not surprising therefore that the most complete (so far) expression of public theology in England should emanate from Bradford.

The 'fresh expressions' movement has not explored the extent to which public theology can be an effective tool for mission. The practice of apologetics – speaking in defence – remains the assumed expression of mission on the public stage. But in a fragmented and contested environment such as we have today we cannot rely solely on an intellectual exercise. To have an impact, the values and practices that public theology promotes have to be 'performed'. Chris Howson in this book moves us way beyond apologetics and demonstrates how public theology can be performed in a way that gains momentum *and* encourages people to follow Jesus. It is important therefore that this book is not just read as a commentary on social action; it is much more than this – it is an example of what David Bosch would call 'holistic ministry'.

Inspiration, intuition and prophetic action are close cousins, and they are rare gifts. However, all of these things have to be shepherded and challenged if they are to remain healthy and in good order. The process that is described in this book describes how this shepherding and honest reflection can take place. The mantle under which such questing and questioning takes place is liberation theology. Such an approach may have its critics, but essentially liberation theology is about questioning and challenging our way of seeing, thinking and doing, and this is much needed in relation to our church life and in the public square. Even so, the stories and incidents that are described in these pages risk being rejected as too political . . . this book courts controversy. Total garages get boycotted as a way of expressing solidarity with the people of Burma, the old Odeon cinema gets embraced by a thousand people, and Chris Howson gets arrested at Faslane. You will find plenty of stories like this here.

This engagement in symbolic action provides the means of high-lighting the values one holds to and wishes to promote. This approach is gaining recognition both here and in the USA. Mobilizing people to take part in 'actions' on issues that trouble them is part and parcel of the 'big society' to which we are being encouraged to contribute. Barack Obama was an 'organizer' of such symbolic actions in Chicago before running for President. However, the 'praxis' that is described in this book has a vital aspect: the commitment to honest reflection and prayerfulness – and genuine recognition of the ever-present hazard of thinking that one's attitude is the only acceptable 'take' on an issue. This makes for a fresh expression of discipleship.

For most churches, worship is the centre of their corporate life, with discipleship left as a private affair. In contrast, the process of Church that is described in these pages puts discipleship and encounter centre stage. This is wise, because worship is a tough proposition for those who only half believe, or have inchoate beliefs, whereas engaging in an issue of concern provides a far more amiable slope towards understanding and responding to Jesus. And more than this, in a postmodern context, people judge things by 'What does it do?', 'What use is it?' Authenticity matters, i.e., do these Christians walk the talk, and to what effect? The actions on behalf of injustice or exclusion are therefore important in giving substance to the message that Jesus is worthy of being followed, and more than this, that Jesus coaches us in different values and practices from the mainstream.

The events and episodes described in this book are all highly participative. People don't hesitate to get involved. Pine and Gilmour[1] in mapping the growth of the *experience economy* give important clues about why this Bradford-based fresh expression of Church is proving to be so attractive. What people, especially young people, want, is a story-rich life, and this is what is on offer in Bradford. Those involved in the events and episodes gain a *narrative of commitment and passion* in their lives, and this exceptional narrative will resonate throughout their lives, continually shaping their decisions and their priorities. This is a powerful and enduring missional outcome.

Chris Howson, in this book, describes how liberation theology can be applied in Britain. However, no theory of action can just be lifted from one continent to another: by necessity, modifications have to be made. In this innovative Bradford experiment I see the following pattern emerging:

Engagement with 'struggle' has become the focus for fellowship and reflection and prayerfulness: could this be described as a process of Church?

---

1 B. Joseph Pine and James H. Gilmour, *The Experience Economy*, Harvard Business School Press: Boston, MA (1999).

Because such engagement always carries the risk of becoming oppositional, and therefore potentially aggressive, a high investment in reflection is required – not least to acknowledge the capacity of those gathered to get things wrong.

In the growing 'experience economy', the episodes and events which characterize such engagement are far more thrilling than accumulating 'stuff' – this in turn helps people to make fewer demands on the earth's resources, and gives expression to be a *more moral self.*

The deep and often traditional resources of the Church nourish commitment, morale and resilience. Engagement in struggle means we *need* to come together as a Church and to be open to God.

Discipleship becomes a total life commitment, and this is contagious.

This business of contagious discipleship is worth pondering further. Many of those involved with Desmond Tutu House in Bradford are students, and I have a hunch that after they complete their studies, many of them will choose to stay in Bradford. They will be reluctant to leave the friends and the commitments they have established in the city through their actions for justice. No doubt they will be subjected to perpetual cries from their parents about how important it is that they get a proper job and pay off their student loans. However, the lifestyle that they will be embracing will be one of commitment to others and to the Creation, giving high value to friendship, and sharing resources and becoming ever more confident in the economy of abundance that Jesus leads us into.

Ann Morisy

Introduction

There are many occasions as a priest when you feel ill prepared for the kinds of challenges that the twenty-first century throws up at you. I was considering this as I lay hidden behind a dense bush, my heart pounding. The zombies were fast approaching, staggering alongside the high security fence of the nuclear facility. I gripped a pillow tightly in both hands and nodded silently to another priest who also lay hidden behind a hedge. We waited until the zombie's moans were nearly upon us before lunging athletically upon the undead enemy. So here I was, outside a nuclear base, engaged in a fierce pillow fight with the hordes from hell. Nothing at theological college had prepared me for this.

The military facility was Aldermaston Atomic Weapons Establishment, and the 'undead' were actually members of the Woodcraft Folk. They were mocking the government's spending on nuclear weapons by dressing up as zombies and singing their support for a future apocalypse. 'Why waste money on the NHS when we are already dead?' said one wearing a ripped overall. The pillows we used to attack these grey-faced young folk were adorned with peace symbols. One read: 'Pillow fighting is the only sane form of conflict'. We had decided to demonstrate the stupidity of war by holding this pillow fight during the 2010 blockade of the Aldermaston base. At one entrance gate several members of SoulSpace, our church in Bradford, were lying on the road, with their hands glued together to form a human chain. This had successfully managed to stop vehicles from entering the base for work. At other gates bishops, Quakers and other faith groups united to pray and chant, while CND members found inventive ways of blocking access to the entrances. SERCO, the company paid to run Britain's nuclear weapons factory, was having a bad week. They were already under increased scrutiny at another of their facilities, the Yarl's Wood Immigration Detention Centre in Bedfordshire. Even the government's own inspectors were calling for Yarl's Wood to be closed following the poor treatment of hundreds of children at the centre. These children had been traumatized by the experience of detention and, worse still, the dawn raid that often preceded it. At this demonstration, some of us were demanding that SERCO should not just stop building weapons of mass destruction – they should also stop detaining innocent children.

This book is a case study of a practical ministry that explores how the Church can stand alongside peacemakers, human rights activists, refugees and all who are seeking justice in our world. It calls on the Church to become more active in the lively and imaginative movements that are working for a more just society and argues the case through the story and experience of a 'fresh expression' church, based at Desmond Tutu House in the city of Bradford.

Since 2005, this church has tried to respond in a contextual way to issues of war and peace, the environmental crisis, the arrival of those seeking sanctuary, and the many other issues of our time. We are trying to build a 'just church', a space that encourages global citizenship and active discipleship.

The book demonstrates that 'prophetic mission', based on principles of liberation theology, can provide a way of doing ministry that offers hope to those both inside and outside the Church, shows solidarity with the oppressed, and is more closely attuned to the needs of local communities. If the Church wishes to be a sign of the reign of God, then it needs to give greater encouragement to ministers and Christians who are trying to live out 'prophetic mission'. One of the ways it could achieve this is by supporting progressive strands within the 'emerging church' scene. In Britain, the fresh expressions movement birthed in the twenty-first century could be a powerful tool for a Church committed to equality and justice.

Over the past five years, I have served as the Anglican city-centre mission priest for Bradford, West Yorkshire. It is a vibrant and resilient city full of determined and holy people. My workplace, Desmond Tutu

House, has become a space for radical collusion between the fresh expressions movement and liberation theology; experimenting to see if the Church can still be relevant and prophetic. One of our projects, JustChurch, has worked collaboratively with Christian Aid, helping young people find effective ways of campaigning for justice and fairness.

The fresh expressions movement is reinventing the Church for a new millennium. It has much to learn from liberation theology, a movement that offers insights into issues of empowerment, context and the nature of society. Liberation theology provides a template for emerging churches to engage with issues of poverty and conflict, a template which encourages serious commitment to the marginalized and disadvantaged.

My own path to discovering the insights of this 'theology of the poor' began as a social work student in the 1990s. Reading the works of Leonardo Boff, Oscar Romero, Margaret Hebblethwaite and Kathy Galloway among many others, I realized that theology was more than just an intellectual and moral pursuit; it could be a concrete and practical instrument for tackling the problems faced by the world's poor. This liberating theology began to influence my social work practice, my life choices and eventually my entire ministry.

In this book I hope to begin a conversation between advocates of the social justice movements and the wider Church, especially those working in modern expressions of Church. It is hoped that this will encourage wider research and experiments in combining social justice with new forms of spirituality.

The first part of the book explains the mechanics and influences behind SoulSpace and JustChurch, two fresh expressions that operate in the city of Bradford. We will look at the movements, the context, the people and the processes that combined to produce a new form of Church that is serious about the task of liberation. The second part of the book explores some of the global and local issues of our times, from climate change to supporting those seeking sanctuary. It will give stories that will hopefully provoke further responses to the challenges faced in the twenty-first century. At the end of each chapter I offer some brief ideas for communities of faith using the headings of Education, Action, Reflection and Sustaining (EARS). This framework, an extension of the 'action/reflection' model, may hopefully be useful to others trying to give shape to a liberating and prophetic ministry.

In the twenty-first century, churches must commit themselves fully to active engagement with the issues of peace, justice and the environment. A renewed and vigorous programme for social change will see our faith becoming relevant again and, as we have seen in Bradford, will attract people back into the Church. The application of a liberating theology will encourage us to build the reign of justice and shalom in the communities in which God has placed us.

All fresh expressions of Church will relate differently to their own particular contexts, but it is hoped that the experiences shared from Desmond Tutu House may offer a model of worship and mission that can be replicated in many other situations. The book encourages new forms of Church to become part of the 'movement of movements' that are working to build another possible world, a world of justice and peace that is in harmony with the values of the kingdom of God. Liberation theology provides the key for allowing Christianity to respond to our modern world, equipping our life and ministry in the modern age.

Part 1

Theology and Praxis, the Shape of Our Story

Chapter 1

Fresh Expressions of Church and Liberation Theology

Liberation theology believes that God is on the side of the poor and oppressed and encourages the Church to participate in creating a new reign of life in which all people live with justice and love. In the 1960s, this theology emerged jointly from the civil rights movement in North America and from some of the poorest and most oppressed communities in the southern hemisphere. It made a brief appearance at the theological colleges of Europe and the United States before it suffered widespread dismissal from all but the most progressive of theological syllabuses. Liberation theology has managed to withstand the onslaughts of bullets and brutal dictatorships, the persecution of ecclesiastical authorities and the contempt of theological institutions. It has survived because it still offers God's response to the realities faced by the poor and persecuted of the world. It is a theology derived not from Marx, but from the Bible's own critique of wealth and poverty. It develops collective responses to inequality based on the teachings of Jesus and the life of the early Christian communities (see Acts 2.44–47, 4.32–37). The growth of unabated global capitalism in the twenty-first century has created much economic disparity, and even in countries where general affluence has increased, the gulf between the rich and the poor has left many communities marginalized and isolated. In the poorer nations, hunger, disease, exclusion, insecurity and vulnerability to human and natural disasters are still the daily experience of the majority of people. Capitalism and consumerism may have brought unbridled wealth to the elite, but, as in all previous empires, the affluence of the few has been built on the suffering of many. The theology of liberation is a response to these inequalities, taking insights from a multiplicity of global contexts. It now encompasses a vast field of theological study and activism including feminist, black, womanist, gay, indigenous, Dalit and Mujerista theologies. A helpful definition is found in Mario Aguilar's introduction to his two-volume work *The History and Politics of Latin American Theology*:

> Liberation theology has become a diversified subject that contains in a theological umbrella of many diverse theologies that use the social metaphor of liberation in order to stand with the marginalized in the name of God and which, through their writings, sustain a defence of human rights and the rights of those in the fringes of society. Their tools include cultural theory, anthropology, history, literary criticism, and mostly a simple way of life that challenges the centrality of profit and consumption within a contemporary capitalistic society and the globalized hedonistic phenomenon of consumerism.

It is this 'simple way of life' that has inspired many Christian communities to try and live out the practicalities of liberation. These churches are active in global peace making and local reconciliation work. They defend the weakest in their communities by providing services for the vulnerable and by campaigning for the rights of the marginalized. Their faith is forever calling them into solidarity with those least able to have their voices heard in local and national arenas. These churches and movements have a keen interest in the issues of global poverty and situations where human rights are being disregarded. The Bible has inspired them to live out ways of being 'good news to the poor' where the mighty are brought low and the humble are lifted up. This biblical vision of the 'reign of God' is combined with a belief that discipleship includes actively challenging oppressive structures. The modern liberation theology movement is driven by the belief that we are called in our daily life to build the kingdom of God on earth as it is in heaven.

Fresh expressions and emerging Church – opportunities and hopes

The 'fresh expressions' movement emerged in Britain at the beginning of the twenty-first century. It grew from Anglican and Methodist faith communities recognizing the limitations of traditional Church in reaching out to those outside Christian circles. It accepts the reality that church attendance and faith adherence is in decline and that the established churches must find imaginative measures to redress the problem. The British official fresh expressions website defines the movement in these terms:

> A fresh expression is a form of church for our changing culture, established primarily for the benefit of people who are not yet members of any church. It will come into being through principles of listening, service, incarnational mission and making disciples; It will have the potential to become a mature expression of church shaped by the gospel and the enduring marks of the church and for its cultural context.

Fresh expressions have begun in almost every part of mainstream British churches with almost 40 per cent of parishes experimenting with new forms of Church, from toddler services to knitting circles. It is not clear how many of these services are fresh expressions as defined above, but there is certainly permission for congregations to push the boundaries and try out new services in different settings. Worship has ventured outdoors to skate-parks, is found in cafés and gyms, and is aimed at groups with defined cultures, from virtual electronic communities to Goths in Cambridge.

Fresh expression churches are often interested in local contexts and want to meet where people are, in cafés, gyms and the like, but the movement also needs to take into account the broader economic political and cultural contexts of our times. The movement has erupted in the period following the terrorist attacks of 9/11 and the subsequent wars and occupations in both Iraq and Afghanistan, yet it has barely been a visible presence in the peace movement. Recently we have seen a growing awareness of the consequences of climate change, but what does the fresh expressions movement have to say about the environment? What does it have to say about the arms trade? What does it think about genocide in Darfur or massacres in the Democratic Republic of Congo? Churches sometimes struggle to respond to such issues, but the fresh expressions movement could help them find a voice. It has the potential to combine the youthful activism of protest movements with the social vision of the gospel.

Contemplation and action

It is clear that the churches have much to learn from wider social movements that are successful in engaging young people in struggles for a fairer society, but what have those movements got to gain from engagement with the churches? The answer may have something to do with the sustainability of campaigning. Activism is a draining experience full of brief highs and awful demoralizing lows. Faith can bring to activism a perspective that can overcome the roller-coaster ride of continual political struggle. Prayer and contemplation can make the difference between 'burn out' and lifelong political resilience. It is important that people who are involved in community transformation learn skills of personal reflection and social stamina. Christianity can offer models of stillness, self-awareness, group solidarity and Sabbath practice which can be of great benefit to those involved in social change. Activists have found great inner strength through the silent or symbolic worship of communities such as Taizé and the Quakers. Time to be still is often missing from mainstream Sunday worship, but the fresh expressions movement has more free-dom in its structure and can make good use of techniques that slow us down and help us reflect. Stillness provides space for wisdom to develop; it sharpens our ability to act decisively. Self-awareness, the understanding of our motivations, strengths and weaknesses, can better prepare us for difficult situations and enables us to watch for signs of stress and tension. In our community we often use the insights of the enneagram, an ancient Sufi technique of revealing hidden motives and compulsions. At least twice a year we hold courses to explore our personality types and how they can help us to understand the driving forces behind our decisions. It is a relatively easy model to use and it helps people to better understand themselves and others. Such psychological tools are useful in working through difficult group dynamics and help us understand why our personalities sometimes clash with others. Without such analysis, much of our energy can be misdirected and non-productive.

In addition to reflective practice and developing self-awareness, churches can provide spaces for social solidarity. From the gathering of the disciples to the base communities of Christians in Brazil, the most effective strategy for sustaining struggle has been building networks of trust and love. To be effective as activists, we need people who know us deeply and will be honest with us. Churches can be excellent places in which to build up such groups of support and solidarity. Shared activities and communal prayer strengthen our collective resources as well as deepen our interior spiritual life.

Finally, churches can create spaces for Sabbath practice. Finding periods for stillness, contemplation and reflection must be prioritized if our activism is to remain healthy. Activists and Christians must be encouraged to take time out. One of the ways in which we model Sabbath time at SoulSpace is by taking the whole of August to relax and have fun. The first weekend of the month is an annual retreat in Whitby where we relax together and enjoy a service on the beach. We don't meet as a Church again until the end of August, gathering at the Greenbelt Christian festival. It is OK to have a summer break! God wants us to be rested and happy. We want to encourage Christians to relax more. I find my local pool and sauna a valuable place, giving me vital space between parenting and ministry. Time spent on sport, journaling, drawing, playing, walking or gardening will keep a person balanced for the long haul. In springtime our church offers a regular activity called 'Breathing Space' which takes people on walks in the countryside. All this encourages us to model a healthy Sabbath practice – time to stop, breathe, reflect and imagine.

Context – cities crying out for justice

Understanding the histories and contexts that we work in is perhaps the single most important key to restoring the relevance of our churches. Researching our local area enables us to understand it more clearly. Hours spent wandering, observing and praying will help us make sense of the spiritual landscape we inhabit. To know God, and to know God's people, we must learn to appreciate and understand the places where we live and not just the bits that we find 'comfortable'. It is in the ignored areas of our towns and cities where we often discover the radical activities of a God working for justice.

The city of Bradford can be an uncomfortable place and certainly endures widespread misconceptions and social stigma. It has had its fair share of pain and trauma, from associations with serial killers to the terrible fire at Valley Parade. The city suffered greatly in the second half of the twentieth century as the woollen, chemical and banking industries collapsed and left a much weakened local economy. Large numbers of workers brought over from Pakistan in the 1970s found that the jobs they had been asked to do had disappeared. Hundreds of mills previously employing tens of thousands of workers lay empty. By the early 1980s, the city was already beginning to have a poor national image and was showing signs of increasing decline. The city had physically deteriorated and suffered from poor planning decisions. Some of its Victorian architectural gems, virtually untouched by the war, were torn down in the 1960s and replaced with ugly buildings. Middle-class people were leaving the city-centre suburbs, creating increasingly marginalized and isolated Asian communities living alongside those unwilling or unable to leave.

On 11 May 1985 the city suffered a horrific blow as a devastating fire broke out in Valley Parade, the city's football stadium. The match against Lincoln City was intended to be a great celebration as Bradford City was to receive the Football League third division trophy, but instead the day was marked with disaster. In the fortieth minute of play, fans at one end of the stadium began to notice flames darting beneath the stands. Soon 56 people had died and 265 supporters were injured, burned or crushed. In a close-knit community such as Bradford, almost every part of the city was touched by the disaster.

In 1989, Bradford hit the television news once again, but this time for a very different reason. The publishing of the book *The Satanic Verses* by Salman Rushdie was deemed offensive by many in the Muslim community and there were calls for it to be banned. A fatwa pronounced in Iran even demanded the author's death. The images of book burnings on the streets of Bradford amid calls for the fatwa to be carried out brought widespread condemnation.

During the summer of 1995, the image of Bradford was to receive another major blow. Tensions between young Muslim men and the local police exploded during July and three days of rioting left the reputation of the city in tatters and parts of the once prosperous Manningham district littered with burnt-out cars and buildings. In 2001, just as the city was picking itself up from the disturbances, the National Front organized a demonstration in the city centre, deliberately trying to cause community unrest. Though the local authorities banned the demonstration, a small group of fascists ignored the ban and began attacking Asian youths in the city streets. The police were perceived as failing to protect local people and soon many young men from the Muslim community began taking their frustrations out on the police. Though the riots were not as protracted as they had been in 1995, the local and national press coverage was devastating and left the city with an uphill struggle to attract investment and rebuild its tarnished image. In the aftermath of the riots many young Asian demonstrators were demonized in the local paper which published hundreds of photos identifying those involved with the riots from the local authority's newly installed CCTV cameras. Unlike previous riots in other British cities, the young men were hunted down, arrested and handed out long prison sentences.

The media, both national and local, seemed to present the idea that Bradford was a hotbed of uncontrollable Muslim youths. Often the talk was of radicalism and fundamentalism. When the terrible events of the London bombings occurred in July 2005, the local paper pasted its front page with the birth certificate of Shehzad Tanweer, responsible for the Aldgate Tube bomb. The headline 'London bomber born in Bradford' ignored the fact that Tanweer had spent most of his life in Beeston, Leeds, and had little to do with the Muslim community in Bradford. A TV drama called *Britz* followed two years later, telling the fictional story of Britain's first female suicide bomber. She was depicted as coming from Bradford, and once again the local Muslim community complained that they were constantly demonized by the media.

As well as struggling to overcome widespread misconceptions about life in the city, Bradford soon had to deal with another dramatic incident. In November 2005, police officers Sharon Beshenivsky and Teresa Millburn responded to a call from a travel agency business near to the Alhambra Theatre. As the unarmed officers arrived at the premises on Morley Street, gunmen burst from the building and shot them both. Teresa Milburn was seriously wounded and Sharon Beshenivsky became the first female police officer to be shot dead since PC Yvonne Fletcher was killed outside the Libyan embassy in 1984. Beshenivsky was a mother of three young children and two stepchildren, and the day of the shooting was the birthday of one of her daughters. It was another terrible tragedy for the city to deal with.

Bradford has also achieved notoriety for a disastrous regeneration scheme that has left a huge hole in the centre of the city, with the council failing to hold to account the developers who had promised a new shopping centre at the heart of the city. The hole is widely seen as representing the terrible problems the city has faced over the past quarter of a century. To top all these social and economic problems, in May 2010 Bradford was once again in the news, this time for the terrible murder of three women who worked in the red-light district. It was an awful reminder of the days when Peter Sutcliffe, known as the Yorkshire Ripper, had stalked the women of West Yorkshire 30 years earlier.

The poor image portrayed by the media is a far cry from the Bradford that those of us who live there have come to know. The city has worked hard to overcome its economic and social disadvantages and has a strength of character that comes from facing up to its problems. Bradford is a city that prides itself on its impressive history of migration, a place that has welcomed countless nationalities: German, Irish, Italian, Polish, Latvian, Ukrainian, Estonian, African Caribbean, Indian, Pakistani, Chilean, Uruguayan, Zimbabwean, Burmese, Iraqi, Congolese and many more besides over the past 150 years. The city has always overcome the difficulties that inevitably occur with such population flows. It is a story of success that other cities could learn from. With its strong faith communities, God lives and breathes here. Certainly it is a city crying out for justice, but it is also a city of radical experiments of living and working. From co-operative resource centres to well-organized squatting movements, from anarchist clubs to churches based on liberation theology, Bradford is a cutting-edge city. The city that birthed the Independent Labour Party following the 1892 Manningham Mills strike has always been a place of struggle and resistance to inequality.

Each city has a hidden past, histories of faith and dissent that are often forgotten and uncelebrated. How do our local churches relate to that radical history? Did they provide meeting places to resist the Poll Tax? Did they help kick out the fascist Black Shirts in the 1930s? Did they blockade Shell petrol stations after the execution of Nigerian human rights activist Ken Saro Wiwa? Was the city a home to the Chartist movement? Did the Suffragettes organize marches in the streets calling for votes for women? Christians need to learn about their city's hidden histories and then find out about more recent struggles. Are groups of environmentalists trying to stop another 'out of town' shopping centre being built on greenbelt land? Who is opposing the privatization of local schools and hospitals? Who is making common spaces available to the community? How are local churches responding to the needs of young people? What are the trade unions up to? Is there a strong peace movement? Who is setting up credit unions? Which people with disabilities are shouting to have their voices heard? Which groups of retired people are demanding pension rights and access to services?

The cities, towns and villages of Britain are full of passionate people changing their communities for the better, and if they are not, they are full of people waiting for the right catalyst for it to happen. The question for our churches is this: how much are they involved in community transformation, and could they play an even greater role in the struggles of local people to build a better world?

Desmond Tutu House and the Victor Jara Liberation Library

SoulSpace is one attempt to be faithful to Christ within the context of local and international struggles for justice and peace. It began meeting in the former Anglican Chaplaincy opposite the university, close to the local college and nightlife of the city. The building has a lively history and houses the world's oldest fair-trade café, now known as the Treehouse Café. It was originally named Michael Ramsey House after the former Archbishop of Canterbury, but as we reopened the House in 2005 it became increasingly clear that the building needed a new name, one that resonated with the type of work we wanted to do. We wanted to name it after a living person of faith who was widely known for social activism. Desmond Tutu came out as a clear contender. He had visited Bradford in 1987, speaking at the local football stadium during a tour building opposition to the apartheid regime. With the ANC (African National Council) banned and its leaders locked up or in exile, Archbishop Tutu had become an important voice of dissent. At the Valley Parade stadium he won over thousands of West Yorkshire people to the struggle for justice in South Africa.

Desmond Tutu is not always a popular figure within modern Anglicanism. Had he retired quietly and been remembered for his part in the rise of democracy within South Africa, he could easily have been seen as a 'safe' saint. His role, though, has been a much more prophetic one. After the fall of the apartheid regime he chaired the truth and reconciliation process, trying to find a new way to bring healing to a nation that had gone through such harrowing violence. The work was fraught with difficulties and met with mixed results, but was later to be held up as a model for nations dealing with the trauma following internal conflict. Tutu continued to cause controversy when he openly criticized the ANC leadership for failing to live up to the expectations of the South African people. He has remained a strong critic of government policies that have failed to deal with the poverty that ravages the majority of the population. He has also dared interfere with the political stories of other nations, notably Zimbabwe and Palestine. In neighbouring Zimbabwe, he has been an outspoken critic of Mugabe's violent regime, and called on South Africa's government to help overthrow him. This was a difficult position to take, as Mugabe was seen as a hero to the ANC movement, playing a pivotal role in supporting the armed wing of the struggle against white rule. In Palestine, Desmond Tutu has named the current situation as a new apartheid. Tutu sees Palestine as a humanitarian disaster and condemns the failure of the global community in holding the Israeli government to account.

Most controversially, Tutu has been a rare international voice against the growing homophobia of the wider Church and has been a constant advocate of an inclusive God. For this reason, he is well respected within the lesbian, gay and bisexual communities and by those within the Church who stand in solidarity with them. Outside of the Church, many who have dismissed religion as oppressive, homophobic and backward, are gently challenged by Tutu to think again. With all this in mind, I asked the then Bishop of Bradford, David James, to write to Desmond Tutu, and ask for permission to use his name for the building in which we work. Much to our delight he wrote back and said yes.

As well as the Café and a quiet peace chapel, Desmond Tutu House houses a small library: a collection of books and magazines designed to share the aims and practices of liberation theology. The library is named after the Chilean musician Victor Jara who first came to the attention of many Christians in the UK through Sheila Cassidy's book *Good Friday People*. Victor Jara played an important role in the 1970–73 government of Salvador Allende, the first Christian Marxist to be elected president in South America. Jara was an idealist, and was determined to work for the benefit of the poor in his country. He joined a seminary, hoping to work for the marginalized from within the Catholic Church. However, he quickly realized that the Church was deeply conservative and heavily aligned to the interests of the powerful oligarchy in his country. The Church happily organized token gestures toward the poor, and had many caring priests, but failed to challenge the system. Jara decided to leave the Church behind, and instead use his musical gifts in the service of the people. He travelled widely, supporting indigenous folk traditions and popularizing the music of ordinary people. He rallied the people to the cause of Salvador Allende's party, which he saw as the real vehicle for change in his society. When Allende was elected in 1970, Jara became a key figure in the cultural life of the country.

The US government was determined to stop Allende's radical socialist agenda from succeeding and spreading to other nations. When it failed to destabilize Chile's government through economic and electoral means (Allende's share of the vote went up in the March 1973 elections), it turned to the military option. The army, led by General Augusto Pinochet, made a coup attempt and bombed the presidential palace. Allende was killed during the storming of the government buildings, but not before making a moving speech to the people of Chile on national radio and negotiating the safe passage of those trapped in the besieged building with him. After the coup, thousands of government supporters, including Jara, were rounded up and taken to the national football stadium which had been turned into an enormous improvised torture chamber. When Pinochet's men realized who Jara was, they smashed all of his fingers so that he would never play his beloved guitar again. A few days later, troops were ordered to shoot him, and his body, riddled with bullets, was later spotted on a rubbish dump.

Victor Jara's music and spirit refused to remain dead and his story was brought to the attention of the world by his wife, the British dancer Joan Jara, and by others fleeing Pinochet's regime such as the nurse Sheila Cassidy. Like Archbishop Romero of El Salvador and thousands of other Latin America Martyrs of the 1970s and 1980s, Jara and his ideals were not extinguished and still continue to inspire hope to the wider world. Their names remind us of one who stood up to the empire long ago, and was prepared to die so that all would be free; in Victor Jara, Romero, Martin Luther King, Gandhi, we find Christ – and we find him very much alive.

Bradford SoulSpace – dialogue with God

When I was appointed as City Centre Mission Priest in 2005, the Bishop of Bradford gave me permission 'to try things out and to make mistakes'. I was not to disappoint him. The task was to set up a series of fresh expressions of Church that embodied a desire to see social change. I looked for partners who shared similar ideals about worship and mission. Alex Jones from Christian Aid helped me to think about a 'JustChurch', a midweek space for people to focus on social justice, and on Sundays we developed 'SoulSpace', a service inspired by the techniques of liberation theology. The hope was to challenge the perception of those who believe that churches rarely involved themselves in issues of social justice and that churches simply replicate or instigate society's problems. For some, the structure of religious life appears deeply hierarchical and mirrors the deep-set inequalities of the outside world. Ritual, processions and clothing speak more of status than of a God of justice. These perceptions of the inequalities at the heart of the Church cannot be easily dismissed. The patriarchal nature of our ecclesiastical institutions has only recently begun to change and women are still marginalized while men dominate the decision-making processes. The long history of institutional racism is also taking time to overcome. John Sentamu's election to the post of Archbishop of York has been a welcome sign of progress but the experience of many black Anglicans and Methodists has been one of exclusion or tokenism. Class inequalities are also quite apparent within the mainstream Churches and clergy from working-class backgrounds are still uncommon. On many levels, the Church reflects many of the disparities in our society, hardly making it attractive to those who wish to change it.

In provision for new forms of worship at Desmond Tutu House, I hoped to learn from the models of Church coming from more progressive voices around the world. New forms of Church are emerging that are rooted in participative and liberating practice. From Iona to Cape Town, God's spirit is experimenting with new ways of inclusive and dialogical worship which are changing the face of the Church. Fresh expressions of worship need to learn from participatory practices that reflect the changes that we wish to see in our communities.

Influences on a just Church

There are many sources that have influenced the way SoulSpace and JustChurch operates, and it is worth spending some time exploring them. Our method of working is presented not because we have an ideal model, but because it is an experiment that might provide clues as to how other dialogical forms of worship might be developed. We seek a conversational Church in which those who attend are listened to and learn alongside each other. It is only from this conversation, this dialogue, that people of faith can move forward in their spirituality and become agents of God's change within the world. Let us look first at the people who have shaped this ministry.

We can say that all the political theologies, the theologies of hope, of revolution, and of liberation, are not worth one act of genuine solidarity with the exploited social classes. They are not worth one act of faith, love and hope, committed – in one way or another – in active participation to liberate humankind from everything that dehumanizes it and prevents it from living according to the will of the father. (Gustavo Gutiérrez)

Gustavo Gutiérrez is widely seen as the 'Godfather' of liberation theology. A Peruvian Catholic priest, he has dedicated his life to serving the poor. His book, *A Theology of Liberation*, influenced a whole generation of academics and church activists who wanted a concrete response to the situations faced by the poor and persecuted. Gutiérrez was one of the theological advisers to the 1967 conference of Latin American Bishops in Medellin, Colombia, and he helped the Catholic Church make brave decisions to stand alongside victims of violence and poverty. Subsequently many Christians in the region faced repression themselves, and discovered what it was to take up the cross and live alongside the persecuted people of Christ. Gutiérrez continues to serve both in academic institutions and as a parish priest in one of the poorest quarters of Lima. His life and work, and that of the thousands of activists and martyrs of the churches of the poor, continually remind us of our gospel priorities. Another leading liberation theologian, Dom Helder Camara, the Brazilian Archbishop and poet, would say at meetings: 'Think of the poorest, most persecuted person you know, and think about how each decision we make will affect their lives.' Liberation ministry means that our first thought is not how to get people to come to church, but to embrace the teachings of Jesus and learn to serve the community with love, especially those battered by poverty and conflict. Only then will our real concern be building the kingdom of God, a place where oppression and persecution are no longer possible.

I was awakened to a radical and egalitarian gospel at the church in which I began my Christian journey. Malcolm King, the parish priest at St Paul's, Egham Hythe, would invite challenging guest preachers such as Kenneth Leech and other advocates of the social gospel, some of whom were involved in the controversial *Faith in the City* report

of the early 1980s, a document which was deeply critical of the policies of the Conservative government of Margaret Thatcher. Our
parish was twinned with a deprived inner-city London estate church
and we had regular exchange visits with them. Church members had
their eyes opened to poverty and deprivation and discovered how the
churches sought to tackle these problems.

I had come from a council estate, and though I left school without
any qualifications, the Revd King encouraged me to return to study at
a progressive local college. At one college politics conference, an MP
called Tony Benn joined the panel of speakers. When asked why he had
become a socialist, he responded by explaining why he had first become
a Christian, influenced by a revolutionary Jesus who sought to change
the world for the better. Afterwards I grabbed his hand, thanked him
and let him know that his comments had greatly helped me to relate my
political outlook with my spiritual one. After college I went on to attend
a social work course at Bradford University but was disappointed that
the profession was so dismissive of issues of faith. Despite faith being a
major contributor to the reason why many people came to study the
course, the secular department saw religion as part of the problem, not
part of the solution. At Bradford I also discovered that the Christian
Union and the local churches I encountered were more concerned with
a strictly personal expression of faith rather than a social gospel. The
emphasis was on adherence to certain dogmatic statements and judg-
ing who was in or out of the 'Christian club'. I failed to see how these
Christians were living out the 'good news to the poor'.

Patrick Curran, the then Anglican Chaplain, introduced me to the
Student Christian Movement. Here I encountered a faith I recognized, and on one of their conferences in London I once again met
Kenneth Leech. His local knowledge and work alongside the vulnerable groups in the East End of London made a deep impact on all of
us on the course. It was also the first time I had encountered openly
gay ministers and Christians, and I was challenged to deal with my
own homophobia, ingrained during my upbringing and assumed in
much of the Christian teaching around me. During a Eucharistic
service in a hospice for those living with AIDS, I experienced the
Holy Spirit in a profound way, and for the first time I was able to
begin to let go of some of my prejudices.

In 1994 Mike Harrison arrived in the University of Bradford and quickly transformed the role of the Anglican Chaplaincy. He formed a strong relationship with the local community, especially those of other faiths, and launched the 'Curry Project' from the basement of the chaplaincy building, providing food for local homeless people cooked by a different faith community each evening. He then turned his energy to setting up the first ever fair-trade café. With money from Christian Aid and Tearfund, he employed a part-time worker to develop the project. His preaching on Sundays was full of wisdom from all faith traditions and he introduced us to the world of Dietrich Bonhoeffer and Vietnamese monk Thich Nhat Hanh. The Methodist Chaplain was equally progressive. Ruth Weston experimented with new forms of collaborative and imaginative worship. Ruth was later to introduce me to the Urban Theology Unit (UTU) in Sheffield and the British Institute for Liberation Theology. During their summer schools I was stretched and inspired by practical theologians such as Janet Lees, Robert Beckford, Andrew Bradstock, Inderjit Bhogal and UTU's director John Vincent. UTU was full of energy and radical ideas and had even developed an Ashram, a place of community living, in the heart of Sheffield. It was to be highly influential to the later development of Desmond Tutu House.

After serving as Student Union president in Bradford I worked as a social worker, first at St George's Crypt in Leeds working with young homeless people, then with Langley House Trust, managing a hostel for people leaving the prison system. Throughout this period I was experimenting with radical communal life in a housing co-op called 'The Hive' in the Manningham area. The calling to ministry would not leave me and I eventually arrived at Cranmer Hall, a theological college in Durham. Stephen Croft was then warden at Cranmer and had a progressive teaching style that was refreshingly participatory. Another lecturer, Chris Hughes from the Catholic seminary at Ushaw, introduced me to the teachings of American social activist Dorothy Day and the ongoing work of the Catholic Worker Movement which Day had founded in the 1930s to offer radical hospitality to victims of the Great Depression.

At Durham I began to explore the possibilities of using the insights of liberation theology in future ministry, and I set up a group called

'The Base', named after the base ecclesial communities of activists and peasants that had sprung up in Latin America in the 1950s and 1960s. In our weekly meetings we experimented with progressive styles of worship and engaged in active discipleship. We travelled to Faslane Naval Base, home of Britain's nuclear weapons system, and began to learn the principles of non-violent direct action. During one blockade of the nuclear base I joined an affinity group from the Iona Community and chained myself to a replica of a Trident nuclear missile. After hours singing and successfully blocking the gate, the police eventually cut me free from the 'lock-on' device and I was arrested. Unsure of the reaction back at college, I was pleasantly surprised by unconditional support from Stephen Croft and my tutor Charles Read. I discovered that a few students had even spent the entire night praying for me during my first time in a police cell.

A week later Robert Beckford, a black theologian from Birmingham, came to give a talk at Cranmer Hall. 'If you are not in trouble with the law, you are probably not doing theology!' he declared and then went through the stories of the prophets, John, Jesus and the early disciples to back up his assertion. It encouraged me to carry on experimenting with ideas of faith and non-violent resistance. Years later I began to encounter other radical contemporaries such as Deacon Dave, Ray Gaston, Keith Hebden and Martin Newell, other priests and deacons involved with non-violent direct action networks.

At college I read the work of Paulo Freire, whose seminal work about education and teaching called *Pedagogy of the Oppressed* had a deep impact on the practice of liberation theology when it was published in the early 1970s. Freire worked on literacy programmes in Brazil and saw dramatic successes while using a revolutionary approach that concentrated on the issues that affected ordinary people's lives. Those in poverty were taught not just to read and write, but to resist and challenge the problems they faced in their daily lives. The programmes helped the people call for governmental reforms, or alerted the wider community to the injustices that they faced. Freire's work highlights the importance of the relationship between teacher and learner: for him, it was the actual process of education itself and not just the content which must be fundamentally liberating. The traditional method, which he termed the 'jug and mug' approach, reinforced inequalities during a process where pupils were simply the receptacles of the teachers' 'outpouring' of knowledge. Instead, Freire proposed a style known as the 'problem-posing' approach, which involved pupil and teacher having a shared learning experience. For Freire, teaching must be completely dialogical, involving participants in the process from the very beginning. It was impossible to start with a traditional approach and expect to introduce a more participatory style later on. Freire wrote that the 'revolutionary' teacher must be 'dialogical from the outset'. In participatory and revolutionary styles of Church, faith leaders must also adopt this approach if they intend to be fully emancipatory.

An early example of the impact of this approach on liberation theology can be found during the 1970s in Solentiname, an archipelago of islands in Nicaragua. This radical community was under the guidance of Ernesto Cardenal, a Catholic priest and poet who later became part of the revolutionary Sandinista government following the overthrow of the Somoza dictatorship in 1979. In Solentiname, the sermon was replaced with discussions by the community of peasants and artists and Cardenal began to record some of these group reflections. His four-volume work, *Gospel in Solentiname*, became a model for a dialogical process throughout Latin America. The interpretation of the Bible stories came from the experience of the people, and the priest or animator's role was to aid the flow of the conversation and act as a facilitator to the discussions.

Changing the style of the sermon was only part of the solution offered by participatory forms of worship. In 2001 a UTU conference looked at how the Bible could be relayed to a new and fast-changing generation. Janet Lees, a United Reformed minister from Sheffield, provoked many with her workshop on 'The Remembered Gospels'. In her church, stories were often remembered collectively and people were encouraged to be imaginative during this community retelling. If they couldn't remember the precise details of events, they were allowed to be experimental and creative. A speech therapist by profession, Lees' fundamental premise was that people could only live out the gospel teachings if they could actually remember them. For that to happen, they needed to be involved in the telling of those stories during the service itself.

As well as exploring participatory ways of telling the gospel stories and democratizing the 'sermon slot', at SoulSpace we also encountered the problem of music during services. Both traditional and modern songs often use language which feels uncomfortable and forces people to sing words which may be patriarchal in nature or expresses beliefs which they simply do not hold. Hymns and modern worship songs are also simply far too long, prolonging the agony of those new to church settings. At SoulSpace we have found the musical styles of Taizé and Iona more helpful. Scottish theologians and liturgists Kathy Galloway and John Bell have helped many of us to discover worship music from around the world that is intelligent, fun and infused with social justice.

Seeking a style of worship which is both mystical and human, we have been influenced by some other unusual sources. The first is American writer and comedian Garrison Keillor, whose Lake Wobegon novels are full of great wisdom and joy. His weekly radio show, *The Prairie Home Companion*, presents a wonderful array of contributions that are thoughtful and uplifting. Our church worship is greatly enriched by the work of this gentle humorist. At the start of each service is an opening monologue directly influenced by the weekly 'News from Lake Wobegon' broadcasts. Another influence is Reverend Gordon Dey, long serving vicar of Tong, in the Diocese of Bradford. As a curate in his parish it was inspirational to be part of services full of laughter in which the priest took great delight in the lives of ordinary people. He was always making small mistakes, only remembering at the last minute to read the banns of marriage, or suddenly thinking a new thought and going off at a tangent. His great compassion for every member of the congregation and his longevity in one of the toughest parishes in the north of England had a big impact on me and on all who served with him.

The final influence on SoulSpace was discovered by the community themselves. To keep in touch with the 'diaspora' of people having to leave Bradford for work and education, one of the most important times of the year for SoulSpace and JustChurch is the Greenbelt Christian Arts and Music Festival held at Cheltenham. We camp together and reflect on the myriad of talks and music on offer. In 2007, many of our community went to listen to the writer John

O'Donohue, and he had an immediate impact on all who heard him. Ranging in subject from birth to death, mysticism to imagination, his theology of beauty intoxicated us. Few speakers can make you ponder, laugh and cry so effortlessly, and each of his poetic sentences could send your thoughts in new and fruitful directions. Members of our community joined the long queues at the sales tent to get a signed copy of his books. Having purchased some recordings of his talks, we listened to them at JustChurch evenings. The resulting discussions were always profoundly moving, and O'Donohue, philosopher and former Catholic priest, teased out many revelations from us: fears, hopes, loves. He made us see the world afresh, and brought the world of mysticism into our lives. Sadly, O'Donohue died a year later of a heart attack, and, upon hearing the news, we spent an evening listening to one of his Greenbelt talks. Tears were spilt as we mourned someone who briefly but deeply touched so many of us. John O'Donohue was particularly important because he opened up the possibility of deeper dialogues with each other. He valued truthful conversations that are not 'merely intersecting monologues' and dared us to reveal our secret thoughts, doubts and hopes. This theologian from Connemara inspired our church towards imagination, beauty and truth.

Saints and spiritual mentors are important to all churches and we need to seek voices from outside who can stir us and help us grow. Churches should seek out the wild voices: poets, activists and anarchists; all who challenge and disturb. We must value those who bravely place themselves honestly before God, encouraging the rest of us to follow.

Chapter 2

Liberating Worship

Having looked at the mentors for the ideology and theology behind SoulSpace and JustChurch, we can now look at the patterns of our worship. Preparing services is a fluid venture and one that is continually being reformed and amended. We plan our services at a weekly meeting called SoulCircle in which the tasks of storytelling, prayers and facilitation are allocated. SoulCircle lies at the heart of the democratic and participatory programme we have created, and we encourage each other to be daring in the form of worship we might use. Apart from the occasional woodland services or experimental art worship, most services take up a familiar pattern.

Gathering the circle

We meet at midday on Sundays at the Delius Centre, a refurbished church building that serves the German Lutheran population of the area. The pews have recently been replaced by chairs, allowing us to meet in a circle formation. The circle encourages a sense of community and embodies our participatory style. As we gather, those present are encouraged to chat to those around them and children can run freely. Contemporary music may be played that has some relevance to the theme of the service. An informal atmosphere is created so that everyone can feel comfortable and relaxed.

After the initial welcome and sharing of notices, the facilitator will give a brief monologue or story of their week before asking everyone to do the same with their neighbours, inviting all to begin the process of listening and sharing. Working in pairs allows everyone to feel part of the dialogical process at an early point in the service. Listening, learning and sharing are encouraged from the outset. Once people have had a chance to speak about their week, they find it easier to express themselves throughout the rest of the service. Members of SoulCircle will sit with anyone new or with someone going through a difficult time who might not want to share their story with a stranger. The sharing of stories is followed by a gathering prayer which reminds us of God's presence through the highs and lows of life. A song then helps us move from our individual experiences to a collective one, often using world music material championed by the Iona Community. After a lively Peruvian *Gloria* we are ready for the Bible story. Working with many people new to church, we only attempt one reading at a time, mostly from one of the four Gospels. We use different techniques of storytelling depending on the particular focus of scripture, but we always avoid reading directly from the Bible. Jesus taught stories in such a way that they could easily be remembered and understood, and the earliest tales of Christ were passed on through an oral tradition allowing people to hear the good news regardless of whether they were literate or not.

The lectionary provides bite-sized portions that are possible to remember and share in this simple way. An annotated version helps make the story more accessible and additional information can be included for clarity, allowing the listener to respond to the full context of the story. Members of SoulSpace take it in turns to tell these stories in their own relaxed style. With no pressure to be 'word perfect', a greater number of people feel willing to have a go themselves. The purpose is not to produce a great piece of theatre every week, but to help people engage with the story. The text is included on the service sheet so that the storytellers' nuances can be challenged and to make it easier for people to reflect on the story. To encourage many people to be part of the storytelling process, we regularly use the 'remembered gospel' techniques championed by Janet Lees. If the story is relatively well known (such as the parable of the prodigal son), we ask everyone to remember what they can about the story in groups of two or three. Then the facilitator helps the groups to share the story to the wider circle. Outrageous thoughts and memories are encouraged, even allowing for different outcomes to the original version, as they can produce surprising and deep insights in themselves. In the *Just Jesus* books by liberation theologians José and María López Vigil, the character of Jesus would sometimes mis-tell stories to provoke a reaction from the disciples. In one chapter, Jesus tells of God being like a shepherd who lets a sheep die in the wilderness rather than risk the safety of the remaining sheep. It is the disciples who are outraged, and argue with Jesus, saying that God would not allow even one animal to suffer and would do all in his power to rescue that sheep! The technique allows deep insights to emerge from texts which have become over familiar. The best theological reflection happens when people feel relaxed enough to say whatever absurd thoughts pop into their heads.

The discussion: listening and learning together

After the Gospel has been shared in some form, the dialogical process continues. The facilitator must resist opening remarks which will limit the conversations. She or he will have plenty of chances to contribute later, but for now the requirement is to facilitate discussions. Sometimes it may be helpful to point out a relevant fact that does not emerge from the story, perhaps a significant relationship to an Old Testament book or a correlation to an earlier event in the Gospel, but on the whole, effort is taken to allow the 'sermon' to emerge from the discussions of the congregation, not from the mouth of the facilitator. Comments made by the facilitator open up the reflecting process of the congregation, never close them down.

The service sheets have three questions on them to help spark conversation. To maximize the dialogical process, and to minimize direction by the facilitator or priest, these three questions are formulated by group consensus at the SoulCircle meeting the week before. The first question will often encourage debate about how the characters in the Bible story may have felt or responded to the situation they found themselves in. The second will be to encourage a discussion about how the story relates to the world around us today. The third encourages a personal reaction. We always remind the congregation that the questions are starting-off points, and that all aspects of the text are open to question. This allows everyone a chance to air difficulties and questions they may have struggled with for many years. A short time for reflection can be introduced to allow people time to gather their thoughts before talking to each other in pairs. The facilitator 'listens out' into the murmurings and may join groups who are struggling in some way. Has the wording of one of the questions caused confusion? Is there someone dominating in a group and failing to allow other people to speak? Those who have attended the preparation at SoulCircle may also intervene to help the discussions to flow.

I am always struck by how thoughtful most people are with each other. It is as if we are so grateful of a space where we are allowed to be heard, that we don't wish to abuse it. I am pleased when friends do not choose to sit near each other, but are prepared to sit with a stranger and learn from a new perspective. Observing a deep conversation between a conservative African student and a liberal gay Christian fills me with great hope. The dialogical process allows for new discoveries to be made.

Prayers: holding our hurts and joys before God

Sharing the biblical passages in such an open way can unleash surprising emotions and reveal difficult issues: domestic violence, poverty, loneliness, despair, bereavement – the whole range of human experience comes to the surface during the process. It is important to follow dialogue with prayer, allowing a space in which we can hold all these thoughts and feelings before God. Prayer must be simple and open, encouraging healing and transformation, allowing people to feel God's solidarity with the hurts and joys of their journeys. Sometimes stillness is all that is required, and as part of ministerial formation, priests should be encouraged to experience the silence held by contemplative orders or at Quaker services. Such communities have learnt the importance of stillness as a vehicle for spiritual growth. A shared silence is helpful for any community that wants to experience compassion and move beyond self-centredness. In quiet prayer all the problems and hurts that have been shared or are still unspoken can be 'held' before God.

A shared activity for prayer can also be helpful: the lighting of candles, writing down prayers and placing them on a cross, or the holding of a stone during a piece of music. Movement and art can also bring something new to the experience of prayer. Individuals respond to prayer in different ways so we use a variety of styles. Faith communities would do well to encourage playfulness in prayer and allow for new ideas and experiences. At SoulSpace we end our prayer time with both the Lord's Prayer and the international prayer for peace. The latter is the closest we get to a 'credal' moment in our service and the words are full of transformation and hope:

> Lead us from death to life,
> from falsehood to truth.
> Lead us from despair to hope,
> from fear to trust.
> Lead us from hate to love,
> from war to peace.
> Let peace fill our hearts,
> our world, our universe.
> Let us dream together, pray together, work together,
> to build one world of peace and justice for all.

The feast of Christ

The sharing of bread and wine can be a moment of great transformation and powerfully connects us with the story of Christ's love, death and resurrection. People come to this moment with widely differing emotions and experiences even if they have never been to church before. Some people find it a fairly exclusive and divisive part of the service. Holding the diversity of God's people together at the Eucharist is hard work and it needs imagination and sensitivity.

We use a variety of styles, from passing the bread and wine around ourselves, to inviting people to come up and 'help themselves' from central or side tables. We have two chalices, one alcoholic and one non-alcoholic – important for people who abstain or for visitors of another faith. All ages are welcomed to partake in some way. We affirm those who choose not to partake and invite them to pray for the life of our work during the Communion. The bread is made weekly by Katrina, one of our youngest members, and a box of grapes is often passed around for all to share, which the children especially find helpful and inclusive. The words we use to accompany this part of the service are mostly borrowed from the Iona Community liturgy as they are both holy and earthly. Inspired by Noel Moules, a theological educator, occasionally the table is overflowing with fruit and wine, reminding us that this 'peace meal' is a reminder about sharing and that God has created enough for all.

Sent by the Lord

A final song is used to signify that we are coming to a close. If the theme has 'stilled us' we will sing something gentle such as a Taizé chant. If something more rousing is required then we will use a lively song from the world Church community such as 'Bambelela' ('Never give up!'), 'Ewe Thina' ('We walk his way') or 'Sent by the Lord Am I'. These SoulSpace favourites reveal a desire for worship which renews and prepares us for transforming the world around us. We end by the sharing of the Peace, and people are encouraged to get to know the names of those they have not met before. Refreshments are served and once a month community issues are discussed and decided upon over a shared meal.

The whole process is built on Paulo Freire's techniques of dialogue, and it is this process, as well as the content, that puts our services in the tradition of liberation theology. Oppressions are exposed and named in the service but it is the dialogical process itself which demonstrates the possibility of change, forcing us to be part of our own liberation. The Bible provokes 'conscientization' as it names the things that bind us and sets us on a course of transformation. Worship brings an encounter with this revolutionary gospel while sharing the experience and struggles of God's people. The dialogical approach brings together people from a wide diversity of backgrounds and encourages them to listen to one another. Listening and sharing becomes the way that the good news of Jesus is proclaimed. In daring our services to be instruments of transformation and by making them as participative as is possible, the power of Christ to transform our lives becomes more visible and concrete. Using these grassroots approaches, church members are rewarded with rich experiences that will strengthen their spiritual journey.

The inclusivity of God

If dialogue is the first concept built into SoulSpace and JustChurch, the second is inclusivity. The inclusive church movement encourages respect and love for all, regardless of class, gender, disability, age, sexual orientation or ethnicity. The history of the wider Church is marred with discrimination, but over the past 50 years many encouraging reforms have taken place, not least the ordination of women in the Anglican Church. This 'opening up' has saved the Church from the disfigurement of patriarchy, although sexism is by no means defeated. Racism is also now openly acknowledged as a problem by the mainstream denominations. Despite black theologians such as John Sentamu, Robert Beckfoot and Joel Edwards who have pushed for change within their different traditions, the procedures and practice of mainstream denominations have failed to eradicate racism within the Church. With regard to issues surrounding disability, the churches are slowly catching up with legislation around issues of access and inclusion, but the noticeable absence of people with disabilities within most existing church structures indicates that obstacles still lie in their way. In terms of class, theological colleges recognize a need to be more representative of the wider community and seek to attract ordinands from working-class backgrounds. The churches are slowly but surely seeking to 'move with God's story of justice and inclusion'. But there is one very obvious exception.

The failure of the mainstream churches to deal with their homophobia and discrimination against the lesbian, gay, bisexual and transgendered communities is one of the biggest obstacles to mission in the present age. It is impossible to convince people that we offer insights into a loving God when we operate a clear system of discrimination and hatred of those who are not heterosexual. I use 'hatred' and 'homophobia' deliberately and provocatively, because as a Church we still stubbornly refuse to understand the impact of our actions. The prejudice of the faith communities is obvious to those outside the Church who encounter it through the media or through personal experience. Unlike changes of attitude seen in issues such as race and gender, the Church seems entrenched in a medieval position on sexuality, failing to recognize that God blesses all who find love, regardless of their sexual orientation. SoulSpace, like many parts of the emerging Church, belongs to the Inclusive Church Network, and seeks to be a place where differences are welcomed and cherished. One member of our community noted at her confirmation service the importance of being affirmed by a gay-friendly church after prolonged experiences of exclusion and discrimination elsewhere. SoulSpace seeks to affirm the strong faith of many gay Christians and challenges the selective use of scripture that distracts from the clear inclusivity of Jesus. Our dialogical approach allows those with more conservative views on homosexuality to be challenged and transformed by hearing the story of gay Christians. We do not expect everyone to share all the same views, but we do expect people to listen to each other, weep with each other and grow with each other. And it is in that process that the radical inclusivity of God becomes known.

Chapter 3

A Just Theology

EARS to hear (Education, Action, Reflection, Sustaining)

A theology of liberation understands God in terms of justice, peace and care for the earth. Through the life and teachings of Jesus and his followers we begin to find ways to challenge oppression and bring about the reign of God. At JustChurch we try to put our thoughts into action. We reflect on what we have learnt at SoulSpace and look at the issues that may have arisen locally and internationally. We have developed a way of working based on four principles: education, action, reflection and sustainability (EARS) and use this as a model to guide our activities.

Education

The concept of 'conscientization' involves educating ourselves and others about the realities of the world. We encourage this through encounter and relationship, and our meetings regularly invite local campaigners to come and share their experiences with us. Every community has its activists and we seek to be a place that is prepared to learn from their struggles. Speakers are encouraged to invite members of JustChurch to get involved with their respective campaigns. While firsthand accounts of campaigning are preferable, documentaries increasingly offer a good way of beginning discussions on contentious issues. Many provocative films and dramas have recently highlighted a wide range of social problems and form a good basis for our discussions about current issues. You can delve into the subject of violence through Michael Moore's *Bowling for Columbine*; overfishing in *End of the Line*; or the problems of climate change in *Age of Stupid*. There is no shortage of films that can encourage a healthy debate about the issues affecting the world. There are also great theological films out there such as the thought-provoking *Son of Man*, a South African retelling of the Gospels, or *Machuca*, exploring the role of the socialist priests in Chile before Pinochet's 1973 coup. A well-made film can really help us to think through what we believe about an issue or inspire us to do something. Members of our church are also encouraged to attend public talks and conferences on faith and justice issues, making good use of the internationally acclaimed Peace Studies department in the University of Bradford. Every year we also attend the Greenbelt festival at Cheltenham as it provides an excellent forum to look at a wide range of global issues. As well as educating our own members, the Church can be an effective place to educate the local community about the issues that matter.

Action

Much effective learning occurs through experience, so it is important that education is followed by action. At our JustChurch sessions, we plan activities that follow on from the talks from activists and visitors. For example, we invited anti-fascist activist Andy Sykes to come to one of our meetings. He joined the British National Party and infiltrated its leadership to expose the violence and hatred of its policies in a secretly filmed BBC documentary. He now faces constant threats from fascists against himself and his family but continues to work in schools and organizations, trying to limit the influence of the far right. Inspired by his actions, we resolved to join him leafleting against the BNP in an area the fascists had targeted during the local government elections. Working alongside groups such as 'Hope Not Hate' and 'Unite Against Fascism' we encouraged people to see that they could play a part in keeping the BNP from winning seats in local elections. In the second part of this book we will explore some other issues that show the relationship between learning and action. From letter writing to direct action, 'praxis' is essential if we are meaningfully engaged with God's historical project for a reign of justice and peace.

Reflection

Activism on its own is not enough. Our work must be informed and rooted in a community of love or we will soon find ourselves 'burnt out'. The activist lifestyle is very demanding, exacerbated recently by the increased criminalization of protest and the cultural marginalization of radical lifestyles. To ensure that action does not lead to a sense of despair, it is vital that reflection is built into the process. Following a JustChurch peace vigil or a demonstration, we always find time to gather and debrief members. This is especially important if there were clashes with members of the public or with the police. The meeting following a demonstration provides an opportunity for group reflection and a chance to share the experience with those who could not attend. We ask questions such as: What felt good about the protest? What felt uncomfortable? Did we manage to do what we set out to achieve? Could it have gone better? We try to ensure that all who participated in the action have a chance to share their personal feelings. Each event is a chance to learn from mistakes, and it is important to spend time encouraging one another, especially supporting anyone who encountered hostility. In a culture where activism has been seen as abnormal, time spent sharing our experiences is crucial. One person may have felt empowered following their arrest, while another may have been wounded by the experience. Some may have felt disappointment or fear or perhaps felt pressurized to do something that they didn't feel ready for. All these matters must be dealt with reflectively and prayerfully before further action can be pursued. At the end of JustChurch meetings there is an act of prayer or meditation. We call for silence and ask people to reflect on the talk, discussion or activity we have concentrated on during the evening. People are asked to think through all they have heard or done during the evening. Even for those without faith this is often described as the most powerful part of the evening.

Sustaining

Sustaining campaigns is a considerable problem. The trouble with 'single issues' is that there are just so many of them! JustChurch members could so easily find themselves bouncing around the vast spectrum of problems faced by the local and international community. They could become 'Rent-a-mob', turning up at the next national demo that comes around, resulting in 'burnout' or pointless and unsustainable activism. If campaigns are worth doing, they need achievable long-term strategies and we need ways of building this into our activities.

One example can be taken from our work with those seeking sanctuary in Britain. After an evening discussing refugees with a visiting speaker, the JustChurch team set up a 'friendship evening' for refugees wishing to improve their English language skills and for those who needed extra support while their asylum case was being heard. Working with this community is demanding and at times heartbreaking, and to keep this project going in the long term, JustChurch invited the local Student Action for Refugees (STAR) group to be joint organizers. The friendship evening has just entered its fourth year, and has supported over 100 people seeking sanctuary in the UK. Working in partnership with other organizations is especially important in sustaining the activities of small groups with limited resources.

While no single tool is for every task, using the model of Education, Action, Reflection and Sustainability (EARS) has been immensely useful in assessing the impact and fruitfulness of our activities. It has provided a process that has deepened our understanding and has reinforced our commitment to the world and its needs.

A place that breathes hope

We need places where activism is seen as normal, places that breathe new optimism into tired problems. We need Church to be a place that helps nurture empowerment, encouraging our members to feel that anything is possible with God. Waiting for governments to act selflessly or restrict the power of big business will be a long wait indeed. Expecting local authorities to respond quickly to the needs of the community is beyond even the best ward councillors and their workers. Hoping ecclesial structures can suddenly be inclusive and world-changing institutions is a little optimistic. Waiting for others to do what God is asking us to do is not the solution. To paraphrase Gandhi, 'We must become the change we want to see in the world.'

Whatever our situation in life, whoever we spend our time with, wherever we go to church or work, it is up to us to use these moments, these contacts, these places, to live out a revolutionary Christian lifestyle. To be a revolutionary is a much maligned term, but it is the right word for our times. We need to 'revolve' (or to use more biblical terms 'repent', meaning 'to turn around') our lives and our world and turn towards the flow of God's hope for each and every one of us. Churches must attempt to be a place where another world is not only possible, but already exists in the lives of their members. We need to create places that breathe hope into our world. This should be the automatic default position of all of our Churches.

A prophetic ministry – protest as mission

The combination of all these threads is a prophetic ministry committed to the kingdom of God. In our lifestyles and worship we are determined to see very real changes in our communities. We strive to be on the side of the poor and marginalized and demand to live in solidarity with the earth and all its peoples.

As a community we see protest as a natural outpouring of the mission of God. The word 'protest' needs to be rescued from its negative connotations. Over the past 25 years or so, the protest movements, from striking miners to environmental activists, have gradually been demonized in the minds of many. A process of systematic criminalization has discredited alternative lifestyles, and the proud heritage of 'protest' is slowly being eroded, especially within the churches. The number of Anglican priests currently involved in non-violent direct action in the UK can be counted on one hand, despite a long tradition of dissent in British clergy, especially within the peace movement. Even a bloody and illegal war in Iraq and the continued occupation of Afghanistan has failed to produce much prophetic outrage from the priesthood. Over a million people are estimated to have been killed in Iraq and Afghanistan since 2003 (precise figures of deaths in both countries are hard to verify, as a decision was taken not to count the bodies of the 'enemy') and in both countries the majority of the population saw us as occupiers rather than liberators. Despite the obvious suffering caused by the wars and occupations since 2001, there was a distinct lack of Christian protest and condemnation. The military and economic destruction in Iraq and Afghanistan was justified by many clergy even though Jesus' commandment to 'love our enemies' probably did not mean to 'blow them into oblivion'.

To protest against violence is a vital part of our faith heritage. We should speak out against the arms industry in general and the nuclear weapons industry in particular. In terms of the environment, it is an obvious and natural Christian position to protest against a carbon culture which is destroying the world that God has asked us to steward and protect. Christians should speak out against all injustices and human rights abuses wherever they occur. We must protest when thousands of innocent lives are cut down in Sri Lanka or Palestine, especially if our governments are allowing the sale of weapons to those responsible. We must protest for a better world than we live in today. Inderjit Bhogal highlighted that protest is a positive choice for all people of faith at the 2009 'City of Sanctuary' annual conference: 'The word is pro-test! Pro, meaning we are "pro" something different, we are "for" something! We are "for" a better, fairer world! "Test" is from the word "testament", a new story, a new vision of how the world could be.'

'Protest as mission' is about using humour, music and joy to confront those with power and reveal the kingdom of God. We invite our enemies to dance with us, to eat with us as in Psalm 23 where heaven is a place where we finally sit down with our traditional foes: 'You spread a table before me in the presence of my enemies.' We invite all to witness a new creation, to see the world through 'resurrection eyes'. Mission is proclaiming the Christ of peace as our Saviour. We put our trust not in Caesar, Obama, Cameron or Clegg but in Jesus Christ.

The biblical case for protest

There is a strong biblical case for a theology of protest, yet it is only relatively recently that academics and scholars have articulated the powerful political and social undercurrents that shape both the Old and New Testaments. Throughout the 1970s and 1980s liberation theologians produced new interpretations of scripture that challenged more traditional understandings of the Bible. These perspectives were often backed up by evidence emerging from the social sciences about the cultural context of Jesus and his contemporaries. Feminist scholars stripped off layers of patriarchal interpretations and revealed a clearer picture of the important role that women played in biblical times. Recently the school of post-colonial theology has done much to demonstrate how the power of imperial culture impacted on the scriptures. From Exodus, the story of resistance to slavery at the hands of the Egyptian empire, to the book of Revelation, steeped in wild and prophetic anger at the evils of the Roman empire, the Bible is shaped in the shadow of imperial domination. New examinations of the life of Christ by academics such as Richard Horsley, Ched Myers and Walter Wink have revealed an activist Christ, whose ministry was one of protest and confrontation with the political authorities of his day, displaying prophetic witness that bears a remarkable resemblance to modern tactics of non-violent direct action. Yet churches are slow to identify with this rebellious Christ, and even dramatic acts of defiance against the state such as upturning the tables in the temple have had their political bite taken out at the pulpit.

For Jesus and his society there was no separation between religious and political spheres, and his ministry was filled with protest and dissent against all who ruled unjustly. He called for the reign of God to usurp the imperial occupation of his land and people. The Roman occupation and the actions of their client rulers shaped Jesus from birth to death. Jesus' infancy narratives begin with the impact of Caesar Augustus's decree that all should pay tribute to Rome. This forces Joseph and his heavily pregnant wife to move to Bethlehem, a town his family presumably had to leave previously for reasons of economic security. The whole story illustrates the cruel hardships forced on a struggling and oppressed people. At his birth, Jesus is proclaimed Messiah, a new leader who will save his people from the rule of tyranny. The violence of imperial oppression is vividly portrayed in the actions of King Herod, who is so fearful of an alternative to his rule that he was prepared to slaughter all the male babies of the villages in the region.

Thirty or so years later, Jesus' mission began in the wake of John the Baptist, a religious and political agitator calling for repentance, a turning away from the nature of imperial culture. John called for radical redistribution of wealth depending on the needs of the people and challenged the corruption of the ruling elite. This eventually led to his execution at the hands of the rich and powerful. Jesus took up his mission, and, through a life of teaching and signs of sharing and transformation, Jesus became the ultimate community activist, freeing people from imperial rule through symbolic acts of healing and exorcism. Occupation had brought hunger and violence to Jewish society and taxes and tithes kept Rome and its client rulers securely in charge. Thousands of men resisted and were killed, leaving a country full of widows and orphans. Within the temptation stories of Jesus in the wilderness, the Devil is portrayed as having power over the 'greatness and splendour' of the nations of the world, a clear indication that the Roman imperialist domain was part of Satan's empire. Jesus' teachings were proclaimed as good news to the poor, in direct contrast with the 'good news' of Caesar and 'Pax Romana', the peace of Rome which merely aided the wealthy and provided a stable market for the trading classes. The Gospel stories are punctuated with references of resistance to empire, with the expectation that the disciples will carry on the way of Christ, even at great risk to themselves.

The Beatitudes in Matthew's and Luke's Gospels display a manifesto for change and demonstrate God's commitment to those who suffer under oppression. They imply that land taken by force from the poor will be returned and that this should be sought through peaceful means. Jesus' teachings are infused with motifs of liberation from oppression. Finally, after stirring up trouble in Jerusalem during the Passover festival, Jesus was arrested, beaten by Roman soldiers and executed on the cross, a death that marked Jesus as a rebel and a threat to the empire. In the words of biblical scholar Richard Horsley:

> The Roman Empire left its marks on Jesus of Nazareth, most obviously on his body. Crucifixion was a Roman form of execution. It was designed to inflict the maximum pain and agony on its victims, by hanging them from a pole or a crossbeam so that they were slowly suffocated to death over a period of many

hours, perhaps even days. The Romans used crucifixion mainly to execute recalcitrant slaves and provincial insurgents against their rule. It was Rome's ultimate way of dishonouring, demeaning, and dehumanizing the victims. Clearly Jesus was crucified. This is assumed in all of our sources. Jesus' followers did not make it up. So it is clear that he was executed by the Romans, not by 'the Jews'. And the inscription on the cross, 'king of the Judeans', indicates why the Romans crucified him. They crucified him as a leader of insurrection against Roman rule.

Post-colonial theology explains the context of imperialism and has given a clearer picture of the relationship between Rome and its client states and rulers. To blame either 'the Jews' or Pontius Pilate for Jesus' death is to misunderstand the way that colonial rule operates. Jesus was a threat to the established order, he was demonstrating that 'another world is possible', and for that claim, the order for his death was inevitable. The killing of Jesus is one in which both imperial powers and its client rulers fully collude. The resurrection story is the most powerful anti-imperial protest of them all. God dismisses the power of Roman tyranny, showing that love and life are greater than those who rule using exploitation and violence. The cross itself is transformed from an instrument of Roman torture into a sign that there is hope beyond the imagination of the oppressors.

Seeing Jesus in his geopolitical location is the only way to make sense of his life and teachings. If we want to follow him we must try to understand the context that shaped him and then see how it mirrors our own. Only then can we begin to learn from Jesus how we ought to respond to equivalent situations today. To take the subject of violence for an example, Jesus' teachings reveal what Walter Wink describes as the 'third way', an alternative to the patterns of fight or flight that have dominated our response to aggression and domination. Instead of submissive approaches (flight) or destructive ones (fight), Jesus advocates a different approach to resisting Roman oppression. Wink demonstrates that passages traditionally seen as encouraging passivity in the face of injustice would have meant quite the reverse in Jesus' time. The teachings in Matthew 5.38–41, 'turning the other cheek', giving your cloak to someone who is suing you for your coat, and 'going the extra mile', are not acts of submission but of non-violent resistance and defiance. The slave master who strikes someone on the right cheek is defied by being offered the left cheek, a sign that the victim is to be treated as an equal. The man suing a poor person for his clothes is publicly shamed in court when that person strips down naked, showing that even the little he has is being taken away. The Roman centurion who can only legally order someone to carry his pack for one mile faces the risk of punishment when the peasant refuses to give up his load after the obligatory mile.

The Gospels are full of these moments of resistance and protest, from old women who constantly pursue the corrupt judges for justice (Luke 18.1–8), to Jesus' blasphemous suggestion that Caesar is not God when asked about paying tribute to the Roman invaders, an event that almost certainly hastened his death (Mark 12.13–17). In the often misunderstood parable of the ten gold coins or 'talents' (Luke 19.11–27), God has been interpreted as the cruel absentee landlord and king who returns from a distant land and punishes those who do not increase his wealth. Jesus, though, is clearly not on the side of such people. Jesus is in conflict with the Roman-appointed client rulers of the towns and cities, such as King Herod. The version of the story seen through the eyes of the poor puts Jesus on the side of the one who buries the money offered to him by the elites, refusing to even take part in the sin of usury. He protests against the powerful king even when he knows the danger of standing up to such a ruler: 'You are a harsh man; you take what you did not deposit, and reap what you did not sow.' Jesus tells this cautionary tale on his way into Jerusalem where he will defy those who have the power of life and death over him, standing before Herod, Pilate and others who 'reap what they do not sow'.

With eyes opened to the stories of protest in the Gospels, we begin to recognize that to follow Christ may mean involvement in resistance to unjust laws and societies. To 'take up our cross' and follow Jesus involves costly discipleship. The scriptures indicate that part of our Christian story is to commit ourselves to a non-violent struggle for peace and justice.

Part 2

Practical Responses to the Issues of Our Time

Chapter 4

The Environment – from Climate Change to Guerilla Gardening

Churches and climate change

If current trends continue, the world will have changed dramatically by 2050. Conflicts over precious resources such as oil and water will have increased. Millions of people may have been displaced by rises in water level, and whole regions may have become unsustainable for human life. The gap between the 'haves and the have nots' will have greatly increased. The rich may be able to protect themselves from some of the problems associated with climate change, while the poor will increasingly be exposed to its horrors. The weather may be more unpredictable and be capable of much greater devastation. Species extinction will be at record levels and the size of natural rainforest cover may be minimal. In short, we may be well on the way to destroying ourselves, yet in the present, we still seem to be in a state of denial. Government policies are still committed to the short-term needs of big business, and individuals are still clinging on to unsustainable lifestyles of car use, air travel and energy consumption. Churches still invest heavily in companies spewing oil into the Gulf of Mexico.

In the Church though, there are signs of awakening to the environmental crisis to come. From the Bishop of London's 'air miles fast', to the work of Operation Noah (a Christian charity devoted to tackling climate change), mission and environmental issues have begun to come together. Various initiatives championed by the work of Christian Ecology Link (CEL) have encouraged places of worship to reflect on their impact on the planet, conduct energy audits and switch to green electricity suppliers.

At Desmond Tutu House our attempts to go green have been small but symbolic. We encourage the use of bikes and foot as the preferred mode of transport to services and events. Having spent my formative years as a road protester, I was intrigued to see if it was possible to resist car culture during my ministry. Even static jobs such as prison or hospital chaplains seem to require a driving licence and our parish system is now so stretched that in rural areas even the keenest cyclist would not be able to cover the distances by bike. In the city, Anglican churches are sometimes 'clustered' making it harder to work on bike and foot within a parish boundary.

During my curacy I discovered the evangelical advantages to environmentalism. The parish had three places of worship, and walking or cycling between them meant being much more available to those outside the church. Moving from brick box to brick box via metal box is not great for mission or for health. Walking also put me on a more equal footing with the local population. Only 30 per cent of the households in that parish, the Holmewood Estate, had a vehicle, and most people used them sparingly because they were expensive to run. Travelling on foot or by bus is an act of solidarity, and on top of that encouraged me to shop locally, further strengthening links in the community. In addition, not having a car meant that I was able to turn our garage into a recycling space for the church and local organizations.

Garages are useful things, and at Desmond Tutu House one of the first things we did was to turn the space into a bike workshop, run by two local squatters and eco-activists. It operated a few days a week until it needed bigger premises and moved to the Bradford Resource Centre. Churches can do a myriad of small things to show their love for the environment: car parks can be reclaimed using homemade raised beds; people on church outings can use public transport and enjoy the countryside without having to rely on the availability of a car. We offer a regular walk called 'Breathing Space' to ensure that those of us living in the city get to enjoy local nature. Spending time together enjoying God's creation is a good way of encouraging the green commitment of any congregation.

Critical mass and guerrilla gardening

In 2009 Chris Carlsson came to Bradford. He was one of the main instigators of the 'critical mass' movement that began in California some twenty years ago. Critical mass is a simple idea: to promote bike use over car culture, you encourage groups of cyclists to converge on a certain street at the same time. The cyclists take over the roads and roundabouts, especially in areas that have been made unsafe for bicycles by unfriendly pro-car policies. Chris gave a talk at the local anarchist club, the '1 in 12 Club' (named in 1981 when then Prime Minister Margaret Thatcher claimed that one in twelve benefit claimants were scroungers). Chris talked about the history of the critical mass movement but also how it had evolved into more organized community resistance to the capitalist lifestyle dominant in the United States. Activists had moved from tactics of simply promoting bike use to forming micro-collectives involved in setting up workers' co-ops, squats and guerrilla gardening schemes.

Guerrilla gardening is the reclaiming of derelict land and putting it to good use. The history of this movement can be traced to the radical reformation, especially in the writings and activities of Gerard Winstanley (1609–76) and the Diggers, who decried the sin of property and declared that 'this earth is a common treasury for all'. More recently, the home of this movement has become Todmorden in West Yorkshire. Gardeners in 'Tod', frustrated by the lack of allotments, had taken to planting vegetables in the roundabouts and on wasteland that nobody was using. Seedbombs (mud, soil and a variety of wildflower seeds) had been thrown over walls into disused barren land, so that wild flowers could grow and attract birds and bees. At first the activities were done at night but now even the local council has accepted the benefits of the scheme and are facilitating participation.

Guerrilla gardening is a must for any inner-city church, and we began experimenting on our street. First we helped clean up the gardens of our neighbours. We posted letters in every door, asking if anyone minded if we entered their gardens to clean up once a week, and we invited everyone to get involved. The street cleaning built up trust before entering the next stage of the plan. We knocked on the doors of the neighbours of four abandoned houses and asked if people wanted to help with a spot of gardening on Sunday afternoons. These four gardens had become wild and unkempt: one had become an area used by local drug dealers, making it a scary place to walk past in the evenings. That Sunday after church, we hacked and cut back the overgrown hedges and cleared the paths. We had asked the local council for gardening gloves, litter-pickers and a 'sharps' container for needles. The church supplied volunteers with secateurs and hedge-clippers. People came out and helped, sometimes meeting their neighbours properly for the first time. On one occasion, a woman threw an impromptu party for everyone involved, thrilled that the garden next door had improved so much. Seeing local people come together and working side by side is a remarkable sight. Guerrilla gardening was doing so much more than just tidying lawns and growing flowers. It was growing friendships.

Next we planted vegetables and flowers in a vacant front garden. Like many de-skilled city dwellers, I have no knowledge of how things grow, so relied heavily on my wife Catriona, who grew up on a farm in South America. We picked a small patch of front garden in a house occupied by refugees, some of whom had helped with previous garden clean-ups. The first big task was to clear the land, and once that was done we planted onions, potatoes and some flowers. One day, we realized that all the onions had disappeared. Later, a refugee called Hamid from one of the flats came round to apologise as he and a friend had used them all for cooking. We were thrilled – it was exactly what we had hoped for, and we invited Hamid to help us when it came to harvesting the potatoes. For a small front garden, we produced a large box full of potatoes which we then distributed down the street.

We then wanted to build some raised beds in our own yard, using bricks we found in a skip. Andrew Dey, one of SoulSpace's keenest gardeners, helped me build a small wall. We drilled several holes into the concrete floor to increase drainage and then filled the beds with compost and soil from the local City Farm. The soil was so fertile that the first batches of lettuces and cauliflower were ready in just six weeks. It was lovely looking out of the window and watching neighbours helping themselves to small amounts of the herbs that we had grown next to the wall.

Guerrilla gardening is quite energy- and time-consuming, yet if you manage to interest the right people in your church, it can take on a life of its own. It also has a knock-on effect on how neighbours perceive the area. After seeing our new garden, an Asian mother managed to dissuade her son from concreting over his front garden and turning it into a car park. Several members of our congregation have now also got involved with nearby community allotments, and have begun experimenting with their own gardens. If churches have their own grounds, they can develop wildflower meadows and encourage other environmentally friendly activities, but if not, guerrilla gardening may just be what your community needs!

Supporting direct action for the environment

The battle against environmental degradation has involved many controversial acts of protest. Climate Camp, a British movement of eco-activists, has played a highly visible role in environmental struggle over the past few years, and has organized gatherings at proposed airport runways (notably the extension to Heathrow), as well as sites for new coal-fired power stations, such as Kingsnorth in Kent. They have even targeted parts of the City of London that are involved in 'carbon trading', a financial scam that allows companies to carry on polluting while appearing to help the environment. Groups such as 'Plane Stupid' and 'Climate Rush' have also pulled off several high-profile actions about climate change. 'Plane Stupid' activists have climbed on to the rooftops of Parliament, unfurling banners proclaiming it to be the HQ for British Aerospace, and even locked themselves onto the wheels of freight aircraft. Another group, 'Climate Rush', organizes imaginative 'flash mobs' at airport terminals causing disruption and spontaneous tea parties. They even stormed Parliament with a thousand women dressed as suffragettes linking struggles past and present. The success of such activities has brought environmental activist groups under the spotlight as never before.

At Kingsnorth, the thousand or so protestors were faced with unprecedented harassment from the 1,500 police officers called in to protect the interests of E.on, the company wanting to develop a new wave of coal mining in Britain. The tactics used to control this demonstration were straight out of combat operations. Helicopters hovered each night over the camp at 2 a.m. and 5 a.m., ensuring that people got little sleep. Toilet facilities were confiscated to make life as unpleasant as possible for the environmentalists. Demonstrators were searched several times when they entered or left the climate camp. Several people were assaulted by police officers for no apparent reason. The ingenuity of protestors in the face of such obstacles is heartening. At a JustChurch meeting just after the event, three members of our church told how they had to leave the camp the night before the main protest, spending the evening travelling in secret. They met up in a local pub, having been told to find a man reading a copy of *Private Eye*. He then told them where to find the lifejackets and paddles that were hidden nearby. Later on, they were led to secret locations where dinghies were concealed in the under-growth. They then paddled towards the power station dressed as pirates!

The cost of policing the demonstration was £5.9 million, and to jus-tify this, the police initially claimed that the protestors were dangerous troublemakers and that over 70 officers had been hurt during the operation. Under 'Freedom of Information' requests, the Liberal Democrat MP Norman Baker later forced Parliament to admit that there were actually only twelve reportable injuries including bee stings, flu and diarrhoea. Throughout the week-long Climate Camp, there had been only four reported clashes with the protestors, all of which were described as minor and resulted in no further action at the time. Such demonstrations are throwing up many concerns about how the state views our right to protest. The film *Taking Liberties* documents the growing criminalization of the peace and environmental protest movement during the Blair years. Under Gordon Brown's short-lived premiership there was no improvement, with the worrying addition of the death of a bystander during the G20 Climate Camp protests in April 2009. The protest had been lighthearted and tremendously effec-tive and the police seemed frustrated at not being able to control the crowds. Many of us on the protest were unnecessarily shoved and struck by batons. It came as no surprise that the actions of officers resulted in the death of Ian Hamilton, an innocent bystander trying to get home during the protest. Police denied responsibility for several days, only releasing a picture of officers supposedly keeping protestors at bay while a man on the ground was given medical attention. They implied that protestors had been obstructive while they were attending someone who needed medical help. Days later the *Guardian* news-paper released footage of Tomlinson being struck from behind with a baton, before being pushed to the ground by an officer in riot gear. Faced with overwhelming evidence, one officer was suspended. There were many other complaints issuing from the G20 protests, backed up by a large amount of photographic evidence. This was despite new legislation that tried to prohibit the photographing of police officers conducting such operations.

Christians have not been a markedly visible presence on many of these protests, with the notable exception of the Student Christian Movement and 'Isaiah 68' activists. For this reason I always wear a dog-collar when on such protests, and am often asked if I am a 'real' vicar by the young people I speak to. It is a terrible shame that they are genuinely surprised that a priest could be involved in these strug-gles for a better earth. Christians should not be deterred from join-ing in with these demonstrations, and should see them as an act of witness. With God's creation facing such cataclysmic disaster, these uncomfortable protests are where some of the most prophetic acts are being performed today. They should inspire Christians to explore new and creative forms of non-violence for the sake of the planet.

Eco-fasting

Defending the planet will mean the churches engaging in practical steps and symbolic actions. One Lent we wanted to do some serious fasting while also wishing to make a statement about God's love for the environment. We decided to try out 'eco-fasting' in which we would give up electricity each Sabbath day. There were to be no lights, just candles; no TV, just live music; no heating, just jumpers; no Facebook, just real conversations. Only freezers and fire alarms were permissible. Travel was restricted to foot, bike and public trans-port, and on each occasion we had to visit a different local wood.

It was tough, especially on my small children who missed their daily session of CBeebies on TV, but it was thought-provoking and even enjoyable for those who took part. Below are some other ideas on how your community might like to get involved in local and inter-national campaigns on the environment.

'Listen then if you have ears!': Commitment to the earth

Education

- Organize a viewing of *The Age of Stupid* or *An Inconvenient Truth* followed by a discussion.
- Contact Christian Ecology Link (CEL) and find out all you can about 'eco-congregations'.
- Invite someone from a pressure group such as Greenpeace to come and talk at one of your meetings.
- Invite someone who has been involved in environmental non-violent direct action to come and talk about how it works.

Action

- Get involved in a local tree-planting session.
- Locate abandoned gardens nearby, clean them up and then get planting.
- Make a map to help publicize all the recycling facilities nearby.
- Give up plastic bags for Lent.
- Organize a 'bike to church' Sunday.
- Do an environmental audit on your church building.

Reflection

- If you have been involved in Non-violent Direct Action, discuss with your faith community how it felt. What impact did it have on those involved or members of the public who witnessed your activity?
- Keep a journal of an eco-fast over Lent or Advent. Look back through the journal and share what has been learnt.
- Meet and discuss stories in the Bible that show God's love for creation.
- What would Jesus' message be to the environmental movement?

Sustaining

- Does your local area have a Friends of the Earth group? If not, could you help form a local group?
- Has your church become an eco-congregation? Could it be part of the Christian Ecology Link movement?
- Organize a regular prayer meeting that focuses primarily on the earth. During such a service personal pledges can be made to demonstrate commitment to protect God's creation.

Chapter 5

The Local Community Context

Churches must have a comprehensive understanding of their local context if they want to build up the kingdom of God. Creating good links with other faith communities enables us to identify common problems and maximizes community resources. At Desmond Tutu House we have endeavoured to build up our local knowledge using a variety of methods. Street surveys allowed us to talk face to face with neighbours and were a good way of finding out the issues that concerned them. Annual street parties (using the Eden Project's 'The Big Lunch' campaign as a model) and open meetings allowed neighbours to get to know each other. Community events such as 'street clean-up' campaigns encouraged a real sense that people can make a difference to local problems. When our church began meeting, we did some 'community mapping' to help us understand our local area. This involves asking the following questions:

- What communities are present in your area? What are their histories? What are the demographics of your region? Which communities are listened to, and which ones feel ignored? Who are the key voices of each community?
- What economic factors impact on your community? How much unemployment is there? Which areas are particularly deprived? Are there any regeneration schemes going on? What are the local amenities like, especially schools, health centres and community centres?
- Which pressure groups and community groups are active in your city or town? Where are the places that communities meet? What

resources are available for people who need support? Where do homeless people go for help? What services are available for refugees, young people or those who are living with HIV/AIDS?

• What are the needs of the city centre? Who defines those needs? What groups of people hang out and where? What is the local authority or policing strategy for the area? What groups represent business or the voluntary sector? Is there an active Trades' Council?

• What are the local churches doing collectively for their area? Is there a 'Churches Together' group? Is it effective? Are there differences of opinions or local rivalries between some churches?

If churches can get a good handle on these questions, then it will be easier to engage in effective community change. With detailed knowledge of what problems a community faces, it becomes possible to build up the relationships and resources to tackle them. Churches should keep an eye on the local press and listen to community radio; they should be constantly talking to people who live and work in the area, especially those from other faith traditions or who are outside familiar circles. Based on real community knowledge, churches should be ready to respond to both the immediate problems that can suddenly occur and the long-term issues that affect a city centre.

Responding to the unexpected

Churches must learn to respond quickly to local and international situations as they arise. Often they are the only group who can help local people find ways of expressing themselves or organizing their response immediately after a trauma or a crisis. Our cities and towns are now so connected to the rest of the world that natural disasters, shootings, conflicts and a whole manner of events worldwide can have local impacts. Vigils, books of condolences, demonstrations, are ways of dealing with events that happen far away. Churches also need to respond to immediate local needs. In Bradford in 2010, the churches found themselves in the centre of a media frenzy following the arrest of a local man charged with the murder of three women in the city. It was important to organize prayer vigils for the victims, prayer walks to express the need for healing on the streets, and emotional support for those caught up in the horror of the situation. It was not the first time local churches had to act quickly following tragedy. Following the death of PC Sharon Beshenivski in 2005, within a month of SoulSpace starting, we were tested in our ability to deal with the harsh realities of city-centre life. The site of the shooting was on the next street from Desmond Tutu House and the surrounding area was cordoned off for a couple of days, with about 40 officers staffing the perimeter at any one time. I contacted the new church members and we made flasks of tea and coffee before heading out into the cold November night. Many of the officers were not prepared for the freezing temperatures and were grateful for the hot drinks. It became apparent that there was a lack of toilet provision so we escorted desperate officers back to Desmond Tutu House throughout the night. By the second and third evenings, facilities had improved, but the tea, coffee and hand-warmers that we provided were still welcomed. These are little things, but in such small acts of compassion God's love becomes real. Following sudden and horrific incidents, churches from Bradford to Whitehaven can really help communities deal with the hurt and pain that inevitably follow.

Challenging top-down regeneration

Urban regeneration is one of the more complex and longer-term issues our cities face. Derelict buildings and urban blight must be addressed, but churches need to be cautious when being asked to participate in such schemes. We should not forget to ask, in whose interest is a regeneration project really for? Will it benefit the local people? Will it have a detrimental effect on some communities? Has there been genuine consultation?

City-centre regeneration involves giving large amounts of public money into the hands of a relatively small number of people: planners, developers, consultants, building companies, property investors. There may be real and well-intended community benefits, arts resources and improved public amenities, yet all too often local communities feel let down by planners and developers. Beautifully presented plans and local facilities often end up not being built at all, or the buildings change in use or design along the way, making communities feel short-changed. In the process of regeneration, much-loved local buildings, areas and resources may be altered or lost completely. People can feel that public money has been wasted or that the benefits are small and only help a tiny minority of people.

In Bradford, the issues of regeneration have been bitterly contested. There is constant media attention on the 'hole at the heart', a part of the city centre that was torn down to build a giant shopping centre. It was due to be finished by 2005, but by 2011 it remains a hole. Most of the community were initially thrilled at the prospect of the development, as it meant that many construction and retail jobs would be coming into the area. The 1960s buildings that had previously dominated the skyline were gone, revealing the beauty of surrounding Victorian buildings. The proposed plans by the Australian developers Westfield looked stunning, and would link up the cathedral quarter back into the heart of the city.

Problems with the scheme soon emerged and the impressive initial designs presented to the public were replaced with much blander proposals. The underground parking had turned out to be too costly and would have to be built on top of the shopping centre, obliterating the Victorian skyline once more. Westfield demanded that the local council spend millions on more 'site preparation'. Local anticipation remained high, with the press firmly supporting the scheme. With all the preparation work finished and the site ready, everything suddenly ground to a halt. The developers began to change the deadlines for when work would actually commence. Westfield had not secured high enough levels of occupation for the shopping centre, and rumours began to be spread of large companies pulling out of the scheme. The local civic society reported that Westfield was approaching local firms and trying to persuade them to relocate to the proposed shopping centre. It was clear that this would have a devastating impact on the existing retail facilities of the city, emptying parts of the historic centre. As the years passed, it looked less and less likely that the local Bradford Regeneration Company and Westfield would do what they had promised. At the tail end of 2008 the whole country faced an economic recession and it looked like the hole was going to be a feature of the city for some time. Huge public outrage followed, culminating in a series of defacements of Westfield's wall inside the city. Many members of the public began to question the whole scheme. Some who had visited other Westfield centres, such as the one in Derby, began to worry about the impact on the city commercially and aesthetically. The hole also meant local people began to enjoy the vistas that had opened up of the Victorian 'Little Germany', an area with the densest number of listed buildings anywhere in the country. Perhaps a park could be placed here, a community resource that reflected the needs of a city with the highest number of young people in the country. The council had advocated a park in the heart for some time, why not have it here?

Westfield had not done as it had promised, and the Bradford Regeneration Company and the local council had failed to hold them to account. On a BBC report into the scandal, local MP Gerry Sutcliffe revealed that the company had secretly offered to opt out of the development, demanding £80 million in compensation. This was a shocking revelation indeed, that a private company could demand such a price for creating a huge wasteland at the centre of a city. The people of Bradford were furious and started making their voices heard. The wall surrounding the hole was filled with beautiful and humorous paintings and poetry. Signs for Westfield were cleverly changed to 'Wastefield'. An anonymous group of artists called 'Spartacus' placed impressive murals around the site, some of gigantic Mr Men appearing from inside. A 'democracy wall' was built, a blank whiteboard for local shoppers to have their say about Westfield. It was not long before the local council workers came to clean off the hundreds of critical comments that were soon written upon it. The council then later came and tore down the 'democracy wall', creating the impression that they didn't want to hear the views of ordinary Bradfordians.

How might a church respond to this sort of regeneration scheme? The Church should avoid the temptation of being quickly drawn into these projects despite regeneration agencies enticing them with private meetings and special consultation events where the wine flows freely. Regeneration agencies may try to make the Church feel like an important stakeholder in a project and attempt to co-opt clergy onto various boards. Once church representatives are seen to be in partnership with a particular scheme, they may find it hard to disassociate themselves from it later if it proves unpopular.

Our role at Desmond Tutu House has been to listen carefully to local people and to support them when they are opposed to the schemes offered by local councillors and regeneration companies. We have been involved with some of the most powerful 'people power' demonstrations that the region has known. As a church we have argued for a park instead of the proposed 'Westfailed' site and have actively campaigned to overturn another controversial regeneration plan: the destruction of the Odeon, a much-loved art deco building in the centre of the city. Our church helped organize a demonstration called 'Hug the Odeon' to remind the local councillors that Bradford people wanted to retain the building and not replace it with yet more unwanted office space and luxury apartments.

The Odeon was built in 1930 as a concert building and dance hall. Though the building lost some of its grandeur in the poor adaption into a cinema and bingo hall in the 1970s and 1980s, it is still a much-loved local landmark. In the city's grand master plan created by Will Alsop in 2001, the significance of the towers was acknowledged and they were included in the original proposals for the city-centre regeneration. In 2003, the public were 'consulted' as to which of three designs they would prefer on the site of the Odeon. Presentations offered either complete demolition or retaining the towers, keeping the original proportions of the building. The latter option was overwhelmingly endorsed by the majority of the thousands who voted in the consultation, though many added that they wished they had also been offered a chance to vote for a complete refurbishment of the Odeon as a large public performance venue. For a long time, Bradford had not attracted large bands and events due to the inadequate size of its main concert space, St George's Hall, and many felt that a refurbished Odeon could be the solution. After extensive public consultation, the Bradford Regeneration Company (BRC) and the public body Yorkshire Forward who had acquired the site, decided to choose a scheme that proposed total demolition of the site and had barely registered any local support. The public consultation had been a farce, one of many to come surrounding the fate of the Odeon building.

Yorkshire Forward, the owners of the site, encouraged the building to fall into a state of decay so that demolition would become inevitable. I found myself meeting with the Bradford Odeon Rescue Group (BORG as it is commonly known) as they wanted to find out what was going on inside the building by conducting their own internal investigation. They needed an independent person to verify whatever they discovered once inside the Odeon. Who better than the city-centre priest?

We met at Desmond Tutu House and dressed in builders' uniforms and helmets before proceeding to the Odeon. We watched out for security guards before removing metal sheets covering a side entrance, then quickly sealed the door behind us. Using torches, we scrambled up through a gap in the ceiling then dropped into the foyer of the old bingo hall. It was as if nothing had changed since the building had closed in 2000. In a scene reminiscent of the film *28 Days Later* we walked around photographing the once majestic interior before heading to the front end of the building. There, on the top floor, we saw that the downpipes at the base of the roof had been severed and now the rain from the roof cascaded into the former entrance area, seeping through the brick walls and destroying much of the facade. We were pleased to see that the two landmark towers remained safe and that many of the interior auditoriums looked as good as new. We discovered that the dance hall's beautiful art deco stained-glass ceiling was still in one piece, concealed but preserved when the building was converted into a cinema. After an entire afternoon exploring the Odeon, I was determined to do all I could to help preserve this splendid edifice.

Over a thousand people came to the 'Hug the Odeon' protest. SoulSpace members brought chalks and encouraged people to graffiti their messages to the council on the pavements and building itself. I nervously thought that many members of the public might find this a bit too daring, but an elderly woman immediately grabbed a stick of coloured chalk and pushed back some barriers to write, 'Save the Odeon, stop destroying my city!' The whole facade was soon full of comments such as, 'I met my husband on this dance floor' and 'We watched the Beatles here!' It was followed by a symbolic hug of the building in which the protestors wrapped themselves around the immense building and car park behind. Surely the local council would listen to this massive outpouring of public affection for the building? The *Telegraph & Argus* downplayed the protest, saying that only a few hundred people had attended. This made them look rather foolish, as many had seen coverage of the protest on the television and it was obvious that there had been much larger numbers at the demonstration. The newspaper had a long history of supporting the claims of the Bradford Regeneration Company instead of local inhabitants. Despite the public support for retaining the building, the council just seemed to become more entrenched in its determination to demolish the Odeon.

At the council planning meetings, the first attempt to demolish the building received over a thousand letters of protest, and the proposed scheme was eventually sunk by English Heritage who opposed it. They felt it disregarded the scale of the vicinity's architecture and asked for retention of at least the facade of the Odeon. Months later the Bradford Regeneration Company redesigned the scheme, but still insisted on complete demolition of the Odeon. In the intervening months they held secret meetings with English Heritage to allay the organization's concerns. It all came to a head in October 2009 in a meeting of the planning committee of the council. It was open to the public, and took representations from the 1,300 people and organizations that opposed the demolition. It was revealed that the planning committee had received only one letter in support for the new scheme. The councillors were then taken on a tour of the interior of the Odeon, and members of the BORG were allowed to go along with them. Back in the council chamber the chair of the meeting asked for a summary of the committee's current position. The public galleries cheered as they heard five of the seven say that they were likely to decide for the retention of the Odeon building. Against the odds, it looked like we would win our case. The legal adviser for Bradford local authority suddenly intervened and outlined that he thought that the councillors were 'not in a sound legal position to oppose demolition'. He demanded to meet with members of the planning committee in private session. Amid angry murmurings from the public galleries, the council members disappeared into a back chamber, returning an hour later. Their mood had changed and when the

vote came, their position was reversed, with the vote being five councillors for demolition and two against. Local democracy took a very
public battering at Bradford City Hall that day.

Not long after, an even bigger public demonstration was held
outside the Odeon. Two brave souls even avoided the security guards
and managed to climb onto the rooftop, securing a huge banner proclaiming 'Save the Odeon'. The demonstration was supported by local
politicians such as John Pennington and David Ward who vented
their disgust at how local democracy had been trampled upon. As
city-centre priest, I addressed the crowds and told them that those
who betrayed the ordinary people of Bradford should be forced to
pay at the ballot box, and in the meantime we should be prepared to
get in the way of the bulldozers. Interestingly, David Ward was
rewarded for his support of local people's causes by becoming a local
MP in the 2010 elections.

Churches must be at the heart of regeneration that argues for
public good before private profit. Families need parks and good play
facilities. People need public places to relax and enjoy themselves in.
In our multi-faith cities people need safe areas in which to encounter
other cultures. The Odeon could provide such a space: a central
swimming pool or fitness centre, or the much-needed home for the
city's unique Peace Museum. The Westfield site could be a stunning
city-centre park, attracting customers back to the city centre and
linking the whole city once more. Churches need to publicly support
ordinary people and demand regeneration that is focused on the real
needs of a community.

Grassroots interfaith work

As well as getting involved with neighbourhood politics and the
affairs of the city itself, those concerned with a city such as Bradford
cannot ignore the issues of faith and race. When looking at education, employment and family life in the city, it is clear that Bradford
faces some particular difficulties. Communities are sometimes segre-
gated from each other by faith and ethnicity, a problem compounded
by issues of class and poverty. Faith and poverty are interrelated.
People have often talked about 'white flight' from Bradford's inner

city, but this is not the full picture. The story has really been one of 'capital flight'. Both white and Asian families have left the inner city when they can afford to, especially as conditions of facilities such as schools have become increasingly poor. It is mainly Asian families on lower incomes who are forced to stay in the inner city, alongside other poor communities such as East European economic migrants and the refugee population.

The complexities of issues and the tensions between these communities need sensitivity from local churches. Churches can feel overwhelmed by such problems, and can even feel under threat. Our priority should be to support each of these communities and begin to address the issues that they face. The starting point is initiating opportunities for dialogue between such communities. Bradford is blessed with a number of such initiatives, from Bradford Churches for Dialogue and Diversity (BCDD) to the 'Faiths Forum'. There are a number of bodies such as the Columba Community who hold monthly interfaith 'prayers for peace', and the 'Concord' group who organize a yearly interfaith walk that introduces local people to the sacred spaces of the different faith communities.

At Desmond Tutu House we introduce those new to Bradford to the groups doing effective interfaith work. We have especially tried to support the work of the interfaith prayers for peace, an initiative which began on the first anniversary of the terrorist attacks on 11 September 2001. A group of Christians and Muslims decided they would meet together to pray for peace. They decided to continue meeting and praying together on the eleventh of every month. On the evening, after a welcome, a prayer from each of eight world religions is read. Silence, the language of God, is interwoven between each prayer. At the end is space for reflections and other prayers in any language. After notices, we retire for a shared meal, normally a traditional Bradford curry. It is often over the meal that God's work of relationship building and friendship making takes place.

Alongside supporting local initiatives such as the monthly prayers for peace, we deal with interfaith matters at a grassroots level. On Ashgrove, our street, we have got to know our neighbours: a concierge from Pakistan, a retired Hindu teacher, a Polish couple who have lived on the street since the end of the Second World War.

We try to get to know one another, and introduce people to their neighbours. I shall never forget the encounter between a Hindu and a Christian who had been neighbours on the same road for over 40 years. They finally had an opportunity to meet at a photographic exhibition held in our community café, and shared many wonderful memories of the area.

The most effective contribution that a church can make to interfaith relations is by facing up to shared problems with neighbours. In 1994, the Revd Mike Harrison, the university chaplain, teamed up with other faith communities to set up the 'Curry Project'. This provided free food to the homeless folk in the area, provided by a different faith group each evening. The project eventually outgrew the chaplaincy building, and is currently housed in a local mosque. The project arose while I was involved in the chaplaincy as a student and remains an excellent model of interfaith work – engaging with a common problem, then getting together with other faiths for a common solution. It is in the working out of such issues that genuine friendships occur and real interfaith work begins. I have less confidence in interfaith schemes that begin without such concrete aims or begin from abstract theological debates.

By organizing peace vigils for Palestine, or inviting anti-war speakers to JustChurch, our building is often packed with members of the local Muslim community. We have shown that we are not out to proselytize, but to learn from each other. We have opened our resources to local people of other faiths who share our concern for the world. Trust takes time to build up. One Muslim woman who had shared her faith story at our church told us that she was told by a friend not to come. 'They are secretly trying to convert you!' she was told. The warning was not unwarranted, as Bradford churches have a history of trying to convert their Muslim neighbours. At many church meetings, Christians are encouraged to make friends with Muslims so as to convert them to 'the one true faith'. Many Muslims feel the same way, and wish to convert their Christian friends to Islam to save them from going to hell. This means that most conversations between our faiths have been, as John O'Donohue puts it: 'two monologues intersecting one another'.

Getting past these hurdles has been helped by a series of initiatives such as the Intercultural Leadership School (ICLS) and the 'Christian Muslim Forum'. The ICLS organizes groups of Christian and Muslim young people to spend a few days together away from their usual environment. They partake in group exercises designed to build up trust, and are encouraged to question each other about their faith. It is surprising to realize how limited our understanding of other faiths really is. Participants have done this twice-yearly in Bradford for over six years, developing good networks of trust. The Forum is a chance for Christians and Muslims to meet every month for a meal together and discuss current affairs or matters of local importance. Once again, trust is built up and transformation takes place over the course of the conversations. Initiatives such as these are rooted in the belief that understanding, respect and acceptance are the principles on which to build real relationships of love and friendship between members of different faiths. The starting point is recognition of our shared humanity, and our faith that God desires the common good. As the saying goes, 'We must take our stumbling blocks and turn them into stepping stones.'

Local politics

Churches cannot ignore their local politicians and should build up a good working knowledge of local government. It is important for us to know our ward councillors and meet regularly with MPs. Communities need to come together if they are to be effective at putting pressure on local decision-makers. Groups such a 'ChangeMakers' and 'London Citizens' have forged strong alliances of local people who then have a much stronger voice in local and national policy. These groups have helped people realize that they do have power and can hold our elected representatives to account. It is crucial that churches teach that power and politics is not just the reserve of politicians. First we must do what we can within our own communities; second, we must make our local representatives accountable for the decisions they take. President Eisenhower is reported to have met with a group of progressive union leaders and nodded in agreement with all the policies that they had proposed. At the end of the meeting he said, 'I agree with you on these things, now go out there and make me do them!' Our job is to make our elected representatives do what we want them to do.

'Listen then if you have ears!': Commitment to your locality

Education

- Do a community survey of your street.
- Go to your local library to find information about your area: what surprised you?
- Collect your local newspaper for a week to see what issues the media focuses on. Do you think it gives an accurate reflection of what is going on in your community?
- Invite a neighbour to come and share his or her story with your church.
- Find out about the nearest five places of worship to your church. Who are the key contacts for them?
- Invite someone involved in interfaith work to come and talk to your group.

Action

- Arrange a visit to your nearest places of worship.
- Organize a community street-clean, or a street party – any excuse to get to know your neighbours!
- Attend a local council meeting and find out who has influence in their party and on local authority committees.
- In your church, decide on a local issue that needs tackling, then follow it up with letters to councillors, local MPs and possible media stunts/direct action.
- Ask candidates from each party to come to a meeting at your church to talk about local and national issues.

Reflection

- Meet to discuss and pray about the problems your community faces.
- Ask a local councillor to give a talk about what drives them.

- Once you have held a community event, reflect on the process of getting neighbours together. What barriers can get in the way?
- In what ways can church help people of other faiths draw closer together?

Sustaining

- Meet to discuss ways in which your church can serve the local community. Which groups might need regular meeting spaces?
- Support existing interfaith prayer initiatives. If there aren't any, is it possible to set one up within your community?
- Can you join in with a citizen's action group such as 'Change-Makers' or 'London Citizens'?

Chapter 6

A Peaceful Church:
Non-violence as a Way of Life

'I'm envious of your hair' laughed Andrei in his broken English. 'In Byelorussian prison, they chopped mine off'; he imitated having his head shaved. Andrei had recently been released from a two-year prison sentence for 'unauthorized' Christian activity in his own country. We were in the Ukraine where I was teaching 'The Principles of Non-violent Direct Action' at a World Student Federation conference. In Belarus, the last dictatorship in Europe, anyone not part of the official Orthodox Church is seen as unpatriotic. Other denominations and faiths are barely tolerated or simply persecuted. If you don't have the right papers from the government then you are not allowed to meet, pray or sing with others, even in your own home. Andrei had been persecuted for his faith but the young man was told that Christians should not resist those with authority. Many of the Christians on the conference were surprised to hear how the Bible can encourage peaceful, non-violent protest. Churches often discouraged them from challenging the state, but as we looked at passage after passage from the Gospels it was clear that the Bible encouraged protest. We met a Jesus who transformed the world and bravely stood up against oppressors. All over the world, Christians are rediscovering the non-violence of God and are daring to show resistance to oppression.

Living out non-violence

Christians who are active peacemakers soon notice the impact they can have on a local community. Desmond Tutu House tries to do this in a number of ways. We provide space for those interested in non-violence and our building houses the Bradford Centre for Non-violence, the Commonweal Children's Peace Library and the regional CND office. We support and co-ordinate those who wish to be involved in national and international peace campaigning and have launched initiatives aimed at promoting non-violence in our immediate community. We are committed to take part in 'concrete' activities that help build peace in our city.

Bradford Street Angels

It is often tempting to think of violence as something that happens in far-off places, in other distant communities. But a great deal of violence happens very close to home: punch-ups outside nightclubs, domestic violence, homophobic or racist attacks. Most of us are fairly blind to the brutality going on in our own communities. Non-violent techniques are effective tools for reducing conflict and successfully promote peace in some of the most dangerous places in the world, so how can we apply these principles to the everyday violence in our cities and towns?

Bradford had a growing reputation as a dangerous place in which to be on a Friday and Saturday night and like many city centres witnesses casual violence on a regular basis. When David James, the then Bishop of Bradford, walked around the city centre with me in 2005, he half joked, 'I want you to be the minister for pubs and clubs!' I travelled to see Christian schemes in various northern cities, but they didn't seem to offer a solution suited to Bradford. I then got an email from a local councillor urging me to go and see what was happening in the nearby town of Halifax. I went over on a Friday night and met up with Paul Blakey, of the Halifax Street Angels. Groups of three or four people would go out in distinctive bright jackets and help out when people needed assistance. They got people taxis, gave reassurance to the general public and generally smiled a lot. They were supported by the town's CCTV system to which they were connected via a radio system. It clearly worked well and I realized that it could work in Bradford.

I travelled over to Halifax again with some friends, Adam Clark and James Clayton, who were also interested in making a difference to the city centre. We began to form a committee of Christians from a wide number of churches, and initiated discussions with the local police and other authorities. It seemed like a huge task to take on, especially as my wife and I found out that we were to become parents for a second time, but God just kept opening doors. First, John Dinsdale, who had knowledge of security issues, joined us on our working group. Then Claudia Powell and Sophie Shaw from the city-centre German Church got involved, and encouraged their small congregation to offer their church as a base for operations. The local 'Hope 2008' offered support, a group based upon a national campaign to bring mission initiatives marked by community action. The city-centre Police Inspector Steve Baker encouraged us and helped secure initial funding with the local council. Finally Chino-Thai, a locally based restaurant, stepped forward with much-needed sponsorship for our uniforms.

Bradford Street Angels launched in December 2007, receiving a great deal of coverage from the regional TV and press media, and it was only a matter of weeks before we won the support of Bradford people. Some police officers were initially concerned about the problems a group of 'do-gooders from churches' might cause. They changed their opinions, however, when we faced our first serious incident. A young man hurdled the barriers on a busy stretch of road in the 'Westend' drinking area of the city and went under the wheels of a passing car. A Street Angel patrol assisted the police officer at the scene but there was little chance of saving the man's life. Witnesses to the horrific incident were traumatized and we brought them back to our base and looked after them until the police were able to do the necessary interviews. The Street Angels staffed the police cordon while the ambulance and fire crew got on with their difficult jobs.

It was an awful incident, but it showed that the Angels could really support the local uniformed officers, as well as give assistance to the general public. Later, the family of the deceased man told us that they were comforted that in his last moments he was surrounded by 'angels'.

After several years of patrolling with over 120 volunteers, the new city-centre Police Inspector, Kevin Pickles, held a press conference praising the Street Angels project. The police revealed that crime had gone down by 22 per cent as a result of the work we had done and physical assaults had been reduced by an even greater amount.

For me, the success of the scheme is down to an ethos of compassion and non-violence. Street Angels works by showing God's love to all, from homeless people to bouncers, from clubbers to police officers. God's love is demonstrated by our desire to bring peace and reduce violence in every situation possible.

Faslane 365

The world's retention of a nuclear threat is still a pressing concern for all concerned with peace. Despite the end of the Cold War, we still face the dire consequences of the potential use of nuclear weapons. President Obama may have won a Nobel Peace Prize, but the nuclear option is not yet off the table. In the UK there are several places that embody the nuclear threat, but none more so than the Faslane naval base, west of the city of Glasgow. It is the home of our Trident nuclear weapons system, the base for our four nuclear-powered and nuclear missile-carrying submarines.

It has been a site of struggle for many decades, but in 2008, as the prospect of the renewal of the Trident system loomed, it became the focus of intense anti-nuclear campaigning. A project was launched called Faslane 365, a year of activities and blockades to highlight the parliamentary vote on renewal of the system. Tony Blair seemed determined to push it through the House of Commons before leaving as Prime Minister.

The Faslane 365 campaign was much more than simply a tool to oppose Trident: it was conceived as an attempt to revitalize the Non-violent Direct Action Movement. Previously at Faslane protests, people had travelled up to Scotland, sung songs, blocked some of the entrances to the base, been arrested and released, but had not done the organizing themselves: it had been left to a dedicated but small group of people within the peace movement. Some of them dreamed up the idea of encouraging visiting groups to take on that work, so that the skills needed to promote peace could be shared by many and could introduce new people to the movement.

When I first heard of the idea, I thought it would be impossible. I met with Sarah Cartin, the then regional officer from CND, and we agonized as to how it could be done. We needed to arrange transport, accommodation and food. We needed to do our own 'legal support', medical training and media liaison. Most of all, we needed to train and prepare enough people from the Bradford region to effectively block a huge nuclear facility. It felt somewhat overwhelming!

We had taken a large contingent of Bradford activists up to the last international blockade at Faslane and everyone was keen to go again. Sarah and I chaired some opening meetings, and tasks were divided, responsibilities for each area were taken by groups, and the preparation began.

I introduced some 'arrestables' (people willing to be arrested during the protest) to 'Dusty', a local artist and a hardened peace activist. I had sketched an idea for a giant 'lock-on' device made from the CND symbol. Three members of JustChurch – Tansy, Lavinia and Ben – went off with Dusty to his warehouse, and started work. 'Lock-ons' simply make it harder for the police to drag you away during a blockade. They normally have to spend a fair amount of time cutting you out of the device before arresting you. The more complicated the 'lock-on', the longer you are potentially able to disrupt the work of the base. The hard part is getting them in place before being arrested, so we hoped that the police would think that the giant CND symbol was just for the cameras. We also constructed a second one, a decoy made of polystyrene that would make them less likely to suspect that one was full of iron rods.

My role in the blockade was media liaison. I would talk to reporters from the press, and had their numbers to hand in my mobile phone. I was not to get arrested, but would relay all that happened to our media contacts.

The evening before, we all travelled up to Glasgow to spend the night at a church hall. One group prepared delicious vegan food for the night and for the early morning breakfast. Despite the secrecy of our plans, two police officers came into the church to find out as much as they could: numbers, ringleaders and the like. When they had gone, we began our training programmes. We did team-building exercises, especially for those who had joined us from Leeds and Huddersfield. We played children's games such as 'Stuck in the mud' (sometimes known as 'Scarecrows') to help us get used to the idea of dodging security guards. We carefully went through the legal framework of what was likely to happen, and how the 'legal observers' would operate. We explained what might happen in the cells, and how to cope with loneliness and other fears. Then people teamed up into smaller 'affinity groups' and drew up their own plans more secretly. Some were chaining themselves together under their clothing; others were dressed in costumes, concealing lock-on devices. Everything was ready for the next day, yet I felt strangely nervous and unprepared. Then one of our church members, Rebecca, asked if we could go and pray. I was surprised at how many came to join us, as we were not all from JustChurch. We sat and offered ourselves to God. We read from Ephesians 6, about putting on the full armour of God. Then silence, followed by deep and powerful prayers about the next day. After this small act of worship, I knew that this was fully of God, and my anxieties were completely lifted. We were physically, mentally, and now spiritually prepared for the events to come.

Before daybreak we wound our way out of Glasgow and towards Helensburgh. One of the affinity groups disappeared off to prepare for the blocking of the Southgate, where base workers often entered to avoid disruptions at the main gate. When we arrived at a car park near the base entrance, we were met with 40 or 50 police officers. It was clear that they were well briefed and prepared, and that we were going to have to act soon if we were to have any chance at all of blocking the entrance. Already, the main gate was busy with traffic heading in for the early morning shift. As we got close enough for us to make a dash for the front gates, I started shouting:

'ONE, TWO, THREE, FOUR' and everyone replied, 'We don't want your nuclear war.' This was repeated until we were in position, then I added the next part of the chant: 'FIVE, SIX, SEVEN, EIGHT. Let's block the base and close those gates!'

The protesters surged forward as the police officers went straight for the CND symbols, obviously realizing that they were our main 'lock-ons'. I could see the first group of police confused when the huge CND symbol that they got hold of was made of nothing but polystyrene! We surged again, and those with the second lock-on quickly rammed their arms into the device and pushed their way off the pavement and onto the road entrance to the base. It wasn't as close as we wanted, but it allowed others with simpler devices to get past the police scrum and get right in front of the gates. It was hard to know what was going on, because I found myself being held by two large police officers.

'I'm standing on the pavement; I'm not part of the blockade, so why are you holding me!' I demanded to know. The officers stood silent. I was supposed to alert the press that Bradford protestors had successfully disrupted the workings of Faslane nuclear submarine base, but I was unable to move. The grip on my arm got tighter. 'Walk with us quietly to the van' one of the officers insisted. I was far away from the protest, and nobody had spotted what was happening to me. 'Over here! I'm being arrested', I shouted to a legal observer. I went limp, making it impossible for the two officers to carry me. Two more officers arrived and I shouted as loudly as I could as I was carried away, to the cheers of other protestors. As I was carried to a police van, I offered a prayer, 'May all here be safe and protected by you O God, anti-nuclear protestors and police alike, for all are created in your image. Amen.'

I was processed in a line of others before entering the van and we sang protest songs and hymns to keep our spirits up. As I went before the charge sergeant I asked again for the reason for my arrest. 'For resisting arrest', he replied. 'But why was I arrested in the first place?' I asked, but there were no further answers.

Once processed, I made my way to the back of the police van. As it filled up, I asked those at the front to talk loudly and distract the officer in the front seat. I still had my mobile phone with all the media contacts on speed-dial. I whispered into the phone, 'Hello, BBC newsroom. This is Revd Chris Howson at the blockade of Faslane nuclear weapons base. I have been arrested and am sending you this live from the back of a police van!' Over the next three-quarters of an hour, I was able to do live broadcasts on BBC Radio Leeds, the Pulse and Real radio, while also giving great material to the *Yorkshire Post* and the Bradford *Telegraph & Argus* newspapers. The arrest had actually helped our media coverage campaign. I used my last call to talk to my wife and reassure her that I was fine and that the blockade had been a huge success.

I prepared myself for custody and was put in a cell with Sam and Paul. Paul was a hardcore atheist and anarchist, and the person I knew least well from the Bradford group. He was young and full of bravado. It was his first arrest. Sam was interested in Hinduism, and had just come back from a year out in Nepal. We were all very different, brought together by our anti-nuclear convictions. Over the next

36 hours in a small cell together we became firm friends. The only problem was who was going to have to use the toilet in the corner first. After many long discussions, one of our final acts before release was to form a human pyramid and make Christian, anarchist and Hindu symbols on the ceiling using bits of paper.

On our return journey from Scotland, we discussed how we could be more successful in blocking the base. I joked that a simpler method of locking-on would be to use superglue to fasten our hands in a human chain. I had been joking, but before long, Tansy, Nina and others from JustChurch began supergluing their fingers together to see how long the effects would last.

Our next blockade, a superglue circle of Bradford activists, was the single most successful closure of the base. The police and security had their cutters ready for chains and D-locks, but were not prepared for superglue. It took them hours to gently wash the hands of the protesters and gradually they were taken away one by one. It was to become the preferred method for hundreds of protestors over the next couple of years, from arms exhibitions to coal-fired power stations. Now, on most protests, the police have a mobile anti-adhesive unit!

Blair pushed through his vote to renew the Trident programme. Though all three Bradford MPs promised me that they would vote against Trident renewal, only Marsha Singh refused to succumb to the bullying of the Labour Party whips. At the end of the 365-day campaign, many of the groups involved went up for one final time. I went with our samba band and kept protestors' spirits high as wave after wave of people found imaginative ways to keep the gates closed to traffic. As soon as one group was removed, others daringly broke through the police lines. Most of our church members were biding their time. In the early hours of the next morning, a colourful Bradford contingent decided to show that the Faslane protests would be carrying on beyond the 365 event. The 'Rainbow block' was met with a completely unprepared security force of just four or five officers. As Nina and five others from JustChurch leapt from their van, they each poured a different coloured bucket of paint over themselves, before dashing towards the entrance. The police officers were not too keen on getting their uniforms ruined, and only one tackled the group. He knocked Nina violently to the ground then angrily dragged her to one side. He taunted her, saying that 'she had failed', and that 'she had let her friends down'. 'We've not failed,' Nina responded, 'we've closed down your stupid base – again!' This tactic may be part of police training, as twice before I've faced similar taunts when being arrested. Quite what they think it will do is beyond me. Thankfully though, Nina was fine, and once more the Bradford posse had resisted the Trident nuclear weapons programme. At the end of the year, over a thousand arrests had been made at the base. Eighteen people connected to our church had been arrested for supporting a nuclear-free world.

Opposing the wars in Iraq and Afghanistan

The 'fresh expressions' movement began at the same time as British involvement in two bloody wars, so perhaps the movement should have a special place in promoting peace as witness to the gospel of Christ.

In Bradford, Desmond Tutu House offered the anti-war movement a base for their activities. Previously, members of the local 'Stop the War' coalition had met all over the place, at the Bradford Resource Centre and members' houses, but now we had a regular monthly meeting time and place. We gained the respect of the local socialist movements and the Asian community, and none of them found any difficulty meeting in a church building. Eventually, when the regional CND office moved in, proudly putting up vast peace symbols on their office windows, Desmond Tutu House became a firm part of the peace movement in Bradford.

The church has a responsibility to highlight the madness of these wars. After 9/11, the United States' foreign policy quickly turned to revenge. The destruction of bases in Afghanistan that may have planned the terrorist attacks was understandable. One could even see the logic of overthrowing the Afghan regime that had tolerated such activities on its soil. But the continued long-term occupation of Afghanistan, endless assaults on the civilian population and imposition of 'client' rulers have inevitably led to bitter resentment from the local people. President Obama has committed a US presence in Afghanistan till at least 2017, but that might easily be extended.

Much money has been spent on war and only a fraction on long-term peace. Instead of a military campaign, an equal amount spent on a 'peace campaign' of jobs, schools and hospitals would change the lives of millions in one of the poorest places on earth. Institutions of peace could be staffed by Afghans, and the only military presence needed would be UN-led. There are no easy solutions to the present situation, but the continued British and US occupation has almost certainly made things worse.

If foreign policy in Afghanistan was a poor response to the 9/11 acts of terrorism, then the war on Iraq was an even more disastrous one. In the build-up to the invasion, we were first told that Saddam Hussein's regime was linked to Al-Qaeda. Then we heard that he was planning a military strike against the West with his 'weapons of mass destruction'. Finally, there were even bizarre claims about the country's nuclear capabilities. Iraq had been a target of US foreign policy long before the planes hit the Pentagon and World Trade Center. Now a fabricated case was being built for an invasion which would give the USA a regional power base and protection of strategic oil reserves. The geo-economic prize of a US foothold in the Middle East, and the destruction of one of the so-called Axis of Evil countries was too great a temptation for the world's superpower. Britain, Spain and Australia were summoned to give an 'international' coalition feel to the invasion despite huge opposition to the war from their respective populations. Millions went on the streets to oppose the build-up of the war. In our city, the Bishop of Bradford spoke movingly to a 3,000-strong rally in Centenary Square. He invited a child onto the platform and held him by the shoulders saying, 'This is what war is about, the lives of children and their families.' Up to two million people marched through the streets of London just before the war broke out, the largest-ever political protest in British history. Horrifically, Blair and others had already made the decision to go to war. Intelligence material which showed that Iraq was certainly not linked to the terrorist atrocities, and did not possess any biological and chemical weapons of mass destruction, was simply ignored. No UN authority had been given, and the legal advice about the legitimacy of the war was clouded by secrecy.

The war broke out on 22 March 2003. Priests such as Ray Gaston blocked main roads in Leeds, reminding angry motorists that it was nothing compared to the horror and disruption our government was causing to lives in Baghdad and Basra. In Bradford, I joined the thousands of schoolchildren who walked out of their schools in protest and massed in the city's Centenary Square. I went on strike for the day, but sadly, most people don't really notice when a priest goes on strike!

I watched the war through the eyes of my good friend Abdullah, an Iraqi refugee who had seen one brother killed by US bombs during the 1991 war. His remaining brother had been imprisoned and then killed under the Saddam regime. Abdullah clearly had no love for Saddam Hussein, but he opposed the destruction and occupation of Iraq. He was convinced that the USA had only one goal, the oil reserves. Sure enough, when the troops went in, they allowed hospitals, homes, museums and businesses to be ransacked, while securely guarding the pipelines and oil facilities.

Local attempts at new democracy were crushed by the USA wanting to instal a leadership of its own choosing. Despite the quick military victory, the following occupation and the deliberate dismantling of Iraqi society led to the bitterest national insurgency since Vietnam. To quell such resistance, there was an equally violent reaction from the occupying troops. The invading forces turned to tactics of abductions, torture and mass imprisonment. Places of resistance such as the city of Falluja saw massive destruction, and local inhabitants were forced to flee. Throughout Iraq, four million people were displaced by the violence.

The late Gene Stoltzfus, founder of the Christian Peacemaker Teams (CPT), came and talked in Bradford about their work in Iraq. With a small team of six, they decided to help out 100 families whose members had been abducted in night or dawn raids. The CPT team contacted the makeshift prisons and eventually were able to locate the prisoners and get messages to the families. It was in these interventions that some of the torture and abuse stories of US-run prisons began to emerge. At first, it seemed too incredible, and the CPT group waited until they and others had more evidence of systematic abuse before helping to expose some of the horrors of prisons like Abu Ghraib.

Conditions for most of the population in Iraq had deteriorated in the years following the occupation, but in the case of the Christian minority, the situation was disastrous. Lydia was a Christian from Basra who studied in Bradford before living with our family for two years, because she felt unable to go home. Through her contacts with family members at home, we knew how poor the conditions were for the ordinary people of Basra. The electricity supply was extremely limited, local facilities hopelessly inadequate and the security of ordinary citizens was negligible. She had wanted Saddam to go, and had even supported the American invasion at the time, but the end result had been devastating on her and her family. Eventually she was forced to return to Iraq, and her fate is unknown.

As a church we helped organize transport to the massive London demonstrations and the huge Manchester protests at the Labour Party Conferences. We took coffins representing British deaths to the recruiting fairs of the British Army, we took children's shoes to the city square to represent the deaths of innocent civilians. We held public meetings about the sale of Iraqi resources to companies such as Halliburton and held regular peace vigils in the city centre.

The most moving vigils I recall were after the abduction of Christian Peacemaker Team members near Baghdad. One of them, Norman Kember, was a visitor to the CPT team in Iraq from the British peace group, the Fellowship of Reconciliation. Kember was taken hostage on 26 November 2005 and was held for four months with three others. Eventually, US citizen Tom Fox was separated from the group and executed. Norman and the others were 'released' on 23 March 2006.

Norman Kember came to speak about his experiences at the CPT British gathering held at Desmond Tutu House. He was humble and jovial, but what struck us all was his unwavering commitment to peaceful solutions, even to his own violent abduction. It was this commitment to peace that made him so frightening to the government. They had tried to discredit him by claiming that he had failed to 'thank' his 'liberators' upon his rescue. This was untrue; he had thanked them endlessly while being released. The smear story in the press was orchestrated by the government and was designed to lessen the impact of Kember's withering critique of the war and occupation of Iraq.

Another prominent speaker, Craig Murray, the former Ambassador for Uzbekistan, also stayed with us at Desmond Tutu House. The British government had forced him out of his post because he spoke out against the torturing of Uzbeks. Murray had become aware that innocent Uzbek citizens were tortured (in one case 'boiled to death') in order to give false evidence that strengthened the US case for invading Iraq. He even took a surgeon to see the corpse of one tortured victim and took photographic evidence. The British government didn't want these stories to be told, as the Uzbek government was an ally in the war against terror, so Murray was discredited and sacked.

Many felt that the churches failed in their duty to speak out after the war broke out. Bishops held their tongues, feeling that they would be compromised should they have to do the funeral services of army servicemen. If our churches had told of a passionate peacemaker called Jesus, who opposed the futility of war, then perhaps all those young people involved in the anti-war movement would have begun to see the relevance of Christ today. In failing to speak out against the war, churches failed to speak out for Jesus.

'Listen then if you have ears!': Commitment to peace and non-violence

Education

- Watch a film about the conflict in Iraq, perhaps *Battle for Haditha*. What does it say about the impact of the war on soldiers and the ordinary people of Iraq?
- Invite someone from CND to come and talk about the impact of nuclear weapons, and current hopes for a non-proliferation treaty.
- Invite someone from the armed forces to come in and share their experiences of serving their country during a time of war.
- Have a discussion in your church about how Christians should respond to violent conflict.
- Ask someone already involved in non-violent direct action to give a training session on non-violence. How might this affect the discipleship in your church?

Action

- If you feel that nuclear and conventional warfare goes against Jesus' teaching of loving your enemy, why not do something

about it? Make contact with the local Stop the War coalition or CND group, and go to the next peace demonstration.
- Arrange a public meeting about the arms trade. Invite political parties to share their views.
- Organize a peace vigil in your city or town centre. Find ways of remembering the casualties of all sides in current conflicts, particularly innocent civilians.
- Write letters about the control of the arms industry. Collect information and materials from Campaign Against Arms Trade.
- Arrange to see your Member of Parliament. Lobby them about government spending on nuclear weaponry.

Reflection
- Have a meeting where members of your church are invited to share their feelings about the wars and occupations that are currently taking place. End the time with worship that allows for times of penitence, silence and personal recommitment to being peacemakers.
- If you have engaged with protest about the conflicts in Iraq and Afghanistan, did you feel it was worthwhile? Did it change anything? If not, why not?
- Do you know anyone who is prepared to be arrested for their beliefs? Reflect as a group on how far your faith might lead you into confrontation with the authorities.
- Spend time with the Bible. In what ways does it justify war? In what ways does it advocate peace and non-violence?

Sustaining
- Ask for your church's commitment to peace to be a regular item on your PCC or monthly church meeting.
- Organize a regular time for people to pray for peace in the world. End each meeting with an action relating to peacemaking.
- Get your church to become a member of the Fellowship of Reconciliation, Christian CND, Pax Christi, the Catholic Worker Movement, Campaign Against Arms Trade (CAAT) or other movements working for peace.

Chapter 7

The Palestine/Israeli Conflict

Shooting the peacemakers

'I think someone you know has been shot' came the message on Facebook, with a link to a newspaper website. I followed the link and saw with horror that one of our former JustChurch members had indeed been shot. In 2008 Bianca Zammit had come from Malta to study at Bradford University and had instantly thrown herself into the non-violence activities of Desmond Tutu House. She had been arrested with us at Faslane, and had joined in with the Palestinian Solidarity Group that operated out of our peace chapel. At JustChurch, she joined in with our letter-writing nights for Amnesty International amid many other bits of campaigning. She was the first to get involved in any activity for peace and justice, and I was not surprised when I received an email from her saying that she was working in Gaza following the Israeli attack on the region. Bianca was part of the International Solidarity Movement, and had been filming a peaceful protest of farmers trying to gain access to their land when an Israeli sniper began to shoot at the demonstrators. As she filmed a Palestinian being tended to by medics, another shot rang out. The bullet ripped through her leg, and extraordinary footage from her own camera witnesses her bravery as she was whisked away and had the bullet wound treated. We sent her messages of support and one month later I received an email from Bianca saying that she had returned to the protests at the farmers' fields the day before – this time on crutches!

The war on the Palestinians and the blockade on Gaza has

seen some terrible atrocities, from the use of illegal weapons on civilians to the killing of nine peace activists on boats bringing aid to the imprisoned population of Gaza. This ongoing tragedy must be addressed more urgently and directly by the wider church community.

A politicizing visit

The Israel and Palestine conflict exists in the background of church life, pushed into the long grass by the weight of practical matters closer to home. The conflict does not often impact on our lives. This changed for me on a trip to Israel in 2005. Organized through a Christian travel agency, the tour was predominantly designed for ministers to see the best tourist sites in the region and then to lead tours to the Holy Land.

The shores of Galilee were stunning and I felt immense joy being in the very landscape where Jesus had walked and ministered. However, as we toured the holy sites of Capernaum and Nazareth I became increasingly aware that something was missing: the story of the Palestinian people themselves.

We had just left Jericho in the Palestinian West Bank and travelled to a site where we were to enjoy a historical replica feast of early Jewish life. After the meal we had the opportunity to ask the local people questions – mostly about practical matters such as transport and accommodation. I asked, 'What is your relationship with the local Palestinians?' The reply shocked me: 'We are Jewish. Jewish people were here long before the Palestinians.' I discovered that the tourist attraction we were visiting happened to fund a local Jewish Settlement, far inside the occupied West Bank territory.

Later, in Jerusalem, I decided to leave the tour group to see a little of the country for myself. Along with some Norwegians who were staying at St George's Anglican Cathedral, I teamed up with Silvi, an 'ecumenical accompanier' from the World Council of Churches. Silvi had been in the country for three months, accompanying Palestinian children on their way to school who were at risk of being stoned by Jewish settlers. As we ventured by public transport to Hebron, I had my first encounter with checkpoints staffed by aggressive Israeli army officers. Hebron is not far from Jerusalem, but in the occupied West Bank, it felt like another world. Walking down into the city centre we found ourselves under a 'ceiling' of steel netting. The netting was littered with bricks, bottles and all sorts of unpleasant rubbish. 'What is this?' I asked. Silvi explained: 'In the heart of the city are the tall buildings in which the 600 Jewish settlers live. They make life hard for the market traders in the streets below by throwing all their waste on them.' The netting was a symbol of cruelty and hate; it was a sight I shall never forget.

Silvi brought us to a tall house just off the market street and she knocked on the door. To my surprise we were greeted by a friendly Scottish voice: 'Come on in, you are most welcome here!' The house belonged to the Christian Peacemaker Team in Hebron, a small group working hard to support the human rights of the local people, fostering reconciliation between all the faith groups. The Christian Peacemaker Team also offers hospitality to those wishing to see for themselves what is going on under Israeli occupation.

When we left the house several hours later, the formerly bustling streets were now empty of traders. Suddenly we saw behind us a group of about 60 people headed our way. 'American Jewish tourists' explained Silvi: 'This will be a "freedom tour" showing Israel's supporters that Hebron really belongs to the Jewish people.'

I tried to engage in conversation with the group, but before there was a chance of a reply, Israeli soldiers approached and angrily shouted at us to get back into the building we had come out from. Silvi and I smiled politely and stood our ground. 'We are just trying to talk to the people here.' One of the officers raised the butt of his gun and pushed us away from the group. It was a frightening and unpleasant situation and a hint of life in the occupied territories. A few days later, a trip to Bethlehem also brought home the reality of it all. Back with the tour group, we entered the birthplace of Christianity through the high prison walls of the so-called 'security fence'. The wall enforces separation of the local community from their farmland and their own people. The wall has encroached deep into the West Bank, and ensures that a Palestinian state can never be viable. The wall is another 'landgrab' for the Israelis, and is a humiliation for the local people. In Bethlehem, the Franciscan Church next to the site of the nativity was being repaired after Israeli soldiers had opened fire on a group of Palestinians. They entered the church thinking that nobody would fire on such a holy place. They were very wrong.

On my penultimate day in Jerusalem I visited Yad Veshem, the Holocaust Museum and Memorial. I joined groups of schoolchildren and army conscripts walking through the exhibition buildings and gardens, and there was silence as visitors took in the horrors of Nazism. In one room a small candle is reflected to infinity by a series of mirrors, while the names and ages of children who died in the concentration camps are read out. I wept and could imagine why the Jewish people were so desperate to find a place of safety in their 'promised land'. Near to Yad Vashem, with no grave markers or memorial tablets, is the site of one of the massacres that took place during the 'Nakba', the killing of hundreds of people in 1948, as Israeli militias drove almost one million Palestinians from their homes. The contradictions of a new home for the Jewish people built on the extermination of another culture are nowhere more obvious than at Yad Veshem.

When I returned to England, I decided that our church must be educated in what is going on. I invited Bridget Rees, the chair of Friends of Sabeel, to come and speak to JustChurch. She was able to help us understand the complexity of the history of the region. Sabeel (literally 'the way' in Arabic) is the liberation theology centre in Jerusalem promoting peace and justice in the region. One of its founders, Naim Atteek, came to speak in Bradford in 2003 and 2010 and explained the situation of Christian Palestinians to local churches and mosques.

Desmond Tutu House became the meeting point of the local Palestine Solidarity Campaign. Many Muslims members had never been in a church building before, and soon friendships began to develop. These relationships became crucial during the crisis that occurred in December 2008. Gaza had been cut off from the world for over two years and the population was driven to increasing desperation and militancy. Elections had put HAMAS firmly in charge of the area. After skirmishes with militants on the border between Gaza and Israel, the Israeli army launched a full-scale assault. Waves of aerial and sea bombardments crushed entire neighbourhoods.

Schools, hospitals, even United Nations warehouses were mercilessly struck. This was followed by a ground offensive, sometimes using weapons banned under international law. There were inevitably many civilian deaths and injuries.

As news of the atrocities came in, I was invited to an emergency meeting at a nearby mosque. We decided to form a group called 'United for Palestine', subsequently known as 'U4P', which would bring together activists from the Stop the War coalition, Friends of Al-Aqsa, the Palestinian Solidarity Campaign and others promoting peace in the region. We quickly organized a demonstration in the city centre allowing local people an opportunity to show their disgust at the bombing of Gaza. The police and local authorities were cautious but allowed us to gather at some playing-fields before marching into the city.

We expected about 300 people to turn up, but by noon, 3,000 Bradfordians filled the park and the local streets. The police and the U4P organizers worked together to steward the unexpected crowds, and the march and rally went peacefully. Our chants promoted peace but showed our anger at the killing of civilians. After the successful rally, the U4P leadership met up again, and we fixed a date for a vigil in Centenary Square outside the City Hall.

The night before the peace vigil I received a phone call from the Archdeacon of Bradford: 'Someone from Bradford Council rang the Bishop's office and asked us to ask you to cancel the peace vigil.' The local council wanted the protests to end and were trying to exert pressure on me through the church. I explained that the vigil was organized by a committee and that it was not in my ability to stop it. The Archdeacon passed on the name of the 'emergency planning officer' who had rung the diocese and I spoke to him directly. It turned out that several people on the council had expressed concern about the militancy of the first demonstration. When they had seen CCTV footage, they did not feel it was a 'mixed representation of the people of Bradford'. As a steward I knew that the initial demonstration was attended by many from local churches and local peace groups, but it sounded as if the council were opposed to demonstrations that appeared to be led by Muslims. They also suggested that the far right might use the demonstration to demand the right to use the city centre for their own rallies. I explained patiently that a peace vigil could not be equated with a BNP rally. The local authorities had long attempted to 'depoliticize the city centre' using the threat of the far right as a smokescreen. The council official insisted that the vigil could not take place, and would personally be there to instruct police officers to forcibly stop it. After our conversation I rang the city-centre Police Inspector. He understood well that Bradford people had a right to have their views heard and that the first demonstration had been peaceful. He assured me that as long as the vigil did not break any laws, it would be allowed to continue.

The vigil, with candles and shoes representing children who were dying in Gaza, was conducted in silence and was completely peaceful. The two police officers who attended were respectful and friendly. The council official who had complained to the diocese did not turn up.

Over the following months U4P held public gatherings giving the latest accounts of the situation in Gaza. The siege of the city remained in place after the withdrawal of Israeli troops so people wanted to help the imprisoned population. Desmond Tutu House became the meeting place of the local 'Viva Palestina' group which eventually took two convoys of supplies to Gaza. Two Bradfordians sailed on the flotilla of aid ships that tried to break the blockade in May 2010, one of whom witnessed the massacre on the flagship vessel *Mavi Marmara*.

As a church, all this has changed our perception of the 'Holy Land'. At Christmas, our nativity set is made from olive wood by Palestinians. The scene portrays the three kings unable to get to the stable, obstructed from the new Messiah by the security wall. Here in the UK, we cannot be blind to the realities of the Israel/Palestine conflict, remembering Jesus without understanding the current context of his native land. Churches can lead the way with the 'Boycott, Disinvestment and Sanctions' campaign, illustrating non-violent ways of challenging the violence of the Israeli state.

'Listen then if you have ears!': A just peace in Palestine

Education

- When they are visiting the UK, invite peace activists such as Jeff Halper and Naim Atteek to share their experiences of the Israeli/Palestine conflict.
- Watch *The Lemon Tree, The Iron Wall* or other films and documentaries about the issue and follow it with a discussion.
- Draw maps of the region to learn where places are. Draw on the changes to borders in 1948 and 1968. Draw the route of the 'security wall' onto these maps. What do these maps reveal?

Action

- At Greenbelt one year, a drama group set up an Israeli checkpoint at one of the gates, refusing a Palestinian woman to pass. Do some street drama to highlight the realities of daily life in Palestine.
- Organize a fact-finding trip to Palestine. Avoid travel agencies that ignore the current situation, instead travel on a study tour with Sabeel or the Amos Trust.
- Join the Palestinian Solidarity Campaign. Find out what's going on and get involved!
- Petition at your local supermarket for a boycott of Israeli goods. The Boycott, Disinvestment and Sanctions campaign is a non-violent way of bringing change to the region.

Reflection

- How 'uncomfortable' is this subject for people of faith? Is there any hope for any reconciliation between differing faiths? What can we do about it?
- Organize a meeting to help members of your church express their feelings on the conflict. How do they feel that Christians should react to the situation?
- Do an exercise in which you place yourselves in the shoes of a Jewish person living in Tel Aviv, a Muslim living in Jerusalem, and a Christian Palestinian living in Gaza. Is it possible to understand their positions?

Sustaining

- Join a group such as Sabeel which are supporting a just peace in the region. When you receive campaigning materials from these groups, ensure it is shared among church members and announced at services.
- See if it is possible to build a link with a church, school or hospital in Palestine.
- Have regular fundraising events for 'Medical Aid for Palestinians' or other such groups. Make sure you sell genuine Palestinian crafts and goods (Zaytoun olive oil is available through the Co-op and social enterprises such as 'Fairgrounds').

Chapter 8

International Solidarity as a Sign of the Reign of God

'When one member suffers, all the members suffer with it. Or when one member is honoured, all the members rejoice with it' (1 Corinthians 12.26).

Access to television and the internet has undoubtedly made the world a smaller place and increased our understanding of events in other countries. Television news bulletins bring us events taking place in countries we may never get the opportunity to visit. Increasing globalization and travel have brought us awareness far beyond our local and national situation. Christians now have greater knowledge of God's world and cannot ignore the plight of those struggling in distant parts of the earth. We are beginning to realize that we are very much connected to these faraway countries. At seminars, I frequently ask participants to take off some of their clothes to find out where the garments are made. Everyone soon realizes that we are connected to workers in Vietnam, Indonesia, Mexico, Portugal and beyond. It is a global village now, and the food, clothes we buy, and the choices of who we bank with and invest in affect people all over the world.

Becoming more aware of the body of Christ globally gives us food for prayer and opportunities for solidarity. As we model our lives on Christ and attempt to take up our cross, we become aware that the crosses of many in our world are very heavy indeed. News of torture, persecution, sweat-shop conditions of labour, war and natural disasters show us the great need to pray and act for God's kingdom on earth.

Liberation theology encourages an active discipleship in solidarity with those around the world. As well as our prayers and fundraising activities to support those affected by war and crisis, we need to increase our understanding of the causes of global events and make links with those in need. Churches should seek out connections with those active in parts of the world where injustice is evident and help their congregations explore the political backdrop of world events.

Solidarity can mean supporting an oppressed group within a particular region, such as campaigns to support Tibetans or the people of Myanmar (commonly known as Burma). Other campaigns such as the Venezuela and Cuba Solidarity aim to provide information about and support for nations who have achieved impressive records of lifting their citizens out of poverty. While not being uncritical of these campaigns and their ideological roots, churches need to learn from these movements of solidarity. If we are to build the reign of God, we must campaign passionately for persecuted communities and should promote the successes of societies that have demonstrated ways of creating equality and justice.

Burma: taking on Total

It was late at night when the doorbell went. I opened the door to a young woman who I recognized from a student union meeting. 'You must help me,' she pleaded desperately, 'they are killing my people.' The woman, a student from Burma, had been watching the defiant scenes from her home land on the television news. It was September 2007 and hundreds of thousands of ordinary people had joined the 'rivers of orange' that walked purposely through the streets of Rangoon. Monks came out in force to oppose the fuel and food price increases that were crippling the people of Burma, and began to call for the release of Aung San Suu Kyi, arrested following her victory in the country's 1990 elections. This confrontation with the military regime could lead to one of two things: a move towards democracy or yet another brutal suppression of the population.

Troops from outside the capital had been brought in and shots had been fired. Deaths were reported, but details were hard to come by due to media restrictions imposed by the Burmese government. Grainy video images taken by mobile phones had been aired that evening and showed evidence of police firing on protestors.

'I cannot be seen to get involved in protesting, terrible things could happen to my family, but could your church do something?' the student pleaded. We hatched a plan using information from the Free Burma Campaign. They were promoting two strategies of non-violent action. First, lobbying governments to impose stricter international sanctions; and second, consumer boycotts of Burmese goods, in particular Total oil. Total, a French-owned company, was the biggest private investor in Burma, pumping huge amounts of revenue into the military regime through shared energy-related projects.

Close to Desmond Tutu House was a garage selling Total petrol so we contacted members of JustChurch and local Amnesty International activists and planned to gather at the university the next day before moving to the petrol station. We invited the local press to come along and used Facebook to publicize the action.

At 12 p.m., 40 people had shown up and we had a quick meeting to see what the group was prepared to do. We decided to close the garage forecourt for a short time and then leaflet cars driving in to fill up with petrol. We were joined by Paddy McGuffin, a reporter from the *Telegraph & Argus*.

Before the protest began, two of us went into the garage to talk to the manager. We wanted to explain why we were there and to reassure him that the protest would be peaceful. I hardly expected him to be pleased but I did not predict the ferocity of his response: 'Me and my mates are gonna get clubs and sticks and beat the sh-t out of you! We'll kill you mother ——s.'

'Thank you for such an articulate quote for our journalist from the *Telegraph & Argus*,' I replied as calmly as I could.

'Could I have your name, sir?' the reporter asked the manager while scribbling on his notepad. The man shouted angrily at us in another language, before grabbing his phone. He thumped the desk angrily and we decided to head back outside. Back with the other protestors I relayed the manager's response and we decided that instead of blockading the garage for a few token minutes, we would now close it down for at least an hour. I went round and helped organize people at the garage entrances.

A police car emerged, and a lone officer came charging at the line of young students, shouting at them to get out of the entrance, and heading straight for the smallest woman. Little did he know that the woman in question was Tansy Newman, one of the most experienced protestors from our church, a veteran of several Faslane blockades. In response to the officer's charge, Tansy simply sat on the ground, whereupon the officer lost his balance and almost fell on top of her. He quickly retreated and at a safe distance called for backup. A picture, taken by the *Telegraph & Argus* reporter, of the policeman pushing Tansy, made the local papers that night. The paper also showed a photo of a Burmese officer attacking (equally non-violent) monks. The story appeared in the *Church Times* with a call to all churches to participate in the boycott of Total petrol until the company had pulled out of Burma.

The wide coverage of the story was largely down to Alison Bogle, the press officer for the Diocese of Bradford, who did her usual thorough job of getting the news out to the most appropriate media outlets available. But not everyone was happy with the coverage. I rang Alison to ask her to help me with another story a few months later and was shocked by what she had to tell me. 'News from your church has effectively been silenced.' She explained that a number of clergy had complained after the Total garage incident, and an emergency meeting of the media committee was held. From now on, news from our church needed to go before a senior member of the committee before being released.

I was stunned. I was offered no chance to explain what had actually happened and nobody had even informed me of the outcome of the meeting. I had no idea that news from our church was being stifled. It was baffling to me that JustChurch's response to the deaths of monks in Burma would create such a backlash from fellow clergy. Later, one priest told me that I was forbidden from ever doing any direct action in his parish. Another explained that the Burmese government should be supported. Others complained that the stories our church generated were not in the interests of the Diocese.

A theology of protest is not going to be embraced by every Christian, and prophetic churches must risk taking bold actions which will not please everyone. Jesus' ministry stirred up lots of controversy and anger, and it is worth remembering that it was the religious authorities that were among the first to take offence at his teaching. Perhaps if you're not in trouble with the church authorities, you're not doing liberation theology.

Prayer flags and petrol pumps

Two years later, at the end of September 2009, a group of us approached the large Total petrol station at the entrance to the M606, the motorway that connects Bradford to the rest of the UK.

We had spent a week collecting prayer flags with individual messages from hundreds of people in Bradford. We wrapped these around the pumps, and occupied the petrol station for a symbolic 64 minutes, remembering that Aung San Suu Kyi had just spent her 64th birthday in detention. The Total manager called the police, but when they arrived, the police were more frustrated with the attitude of the Total staff than with the peaceful protesters. The colourful Buddhist prayer flags were very effective at getting our message across and many drivers were genuinely surprised to hear of the link between Total and Burma.

The action had wonderful and unexpected consequences. A few days later I received a phone call from a representative of the local Burmese community who had seen the protest on the news and was thrilled that people were taking a stand on the affairs of their country. I was invited to the homes of several members of the community, and was delighted to see newspaper clippings of our activities decorating the walls!

These individuals were members of the Burmese Rohingya community, a group heavily persecuted following the 1990 military crackdown. The Rohingyas, a Muslim minority, had lost their property and citizenship rights and were sometimes used as slave labour. In the past twenty years over one million of them were forced out of Burma, fleeing into refugee camps in Bangladesh. The conditions in these camps are so terrible that the United Nations are now trying to house some of them in other parts of the world, including England. The Bradford Rohingyas were touched by our small act of solidarity and now work with JustChurch, highlighting the continued plight of the Burmese people. Our church's growing friendships with these Muslim refugees is a sign of God's kingdom, of solidarity between all faiths, united in the cause of peace and justice.

Latin American solidarity

If defending monks in Burma causes controversy, then solidarity with the peoples and progressive governments of Cuba and Venezuela is bound to be even more problematic. The notion of holding up Cuba or Venezuela as model nations does not sit well with many Christians. Alleged Cuban persecution of Christians is often cited, while Venezuela's president Hugo Chavez is portrayed in the international media as a despotic lunatic. Both countries, however, have impressive track records of serving the needs of the poor. They have fought for greater redistribution of wealth, and have implemented successful education and health-care policies enviable in much richer economies. While externally seen as 'enemies of democracy', they have achieved high levels of internal legitimacy and each fought off coups supported by US foreign policy. Cuba and Venezuela have encouraged a renewal of socialism in Latin America and leftist governments have been elected in Uruguay, Argentina, Chile, Brazil, Ecuador, Bolivia and Nicaragua since 2001. In April 2008, Fernando Lugo, a former Catholic Bishop and liberation theologian, was elected president of Paraguay, ending 61 years of conservative control.

Naomi Klein's book *The Shock Doctrine* describes the hope witnessed throughout Latin America as the twin shocks of military violence and economic neo-liberalism are finally being shaken off. Countries that suffered brutal national security states in the 1970s and 1980s, in which hundreds of thousands of trade unionists, academics and Christians were murdered or fled into exile, are now seeing a return to democratic socialism. The military coup in Honduras in 2009 is a sign that right-wing despotism has not totally been defeated, but the gains of the left across the region have nevertheless been considerable. Venezuela and Cuba have played a pivotal role in the emergence of a viable alternative to free market capitalism, much to the annoyance of Western governments.

I have a strong affinity towards Cuba and was even given a clerical shirt with a picture of Che Guevara as a present when finishing my curacy! I was ordained by Cuban Bishop Miguel Tamayo during his visit to Bradford in 2003. When I asked Miguel about state repression of the churches, he replied, 'It is only churches that are involved in

destabilising the state that fear the government.' These churches sometimes receive their funds from the USA and promote a God who hates
Castro and loves capitalism. In truth, many churches thrive under
Cuban communism, which has never tried to force atheism on its
people, unlike Soviet versions of communism. Castro, while personally
dismissive of the trappings of organized religion, openly supported the
liberation theology movement as a force for the improvement of society.

At JustChurch, we have hosted several speakers from Cuba to try
and rebalance the public debate about their situation. While the
Cuban government does have a questionable human rights record,
that must be seen in the light of constant efforts by the USA to overthrow the regime. After the failed Bay of Pigs invasion, the CIA
engaged in hundreds of attempts to assassinate Fidel Castro and
destabilize the nation. Despite this they have worked hard to eradicate hunger and illiteracy, not just in their own country but throughout the region and beyond.

What's so good about Cuba?

Cuba demonstrates an alternative to the Western capitalist model.
Castro has stood up for the poorest nations of the world, speaking up
against international debt and the policies of the IMF and World
Bank. Cuba has a defiant internationalism, even sending soldiers to
defend Angola against the South African apartheid regime. In terms
of health care, Cuba has more doctors operating around the globe
than the World Health Organization. In Montevideo, the Uruguayan
capital, my wife and I met Cuban doctors working in some of the
poorest parts of the city treating people living with HIV infection.

Education in Cuba is free, not just for its own people but to
thousands from neighbouring countries. In our church we met a
Caribbean student who came to do her MA in England, having spent
two years studying at a Cuban university. In Havana, tuition, housing
and food had been free. By contrast, by the time she left Britain, she
was £17,000 in debt. She also told us the standard of teaching had
been much higher in Cuba.

In terms of the environment, Havana has become a champion of
sustainability, locally growing half of the city's food requirements. It

has also become a world manufacturer of affordable drugs to combat common diseases. It has achieved all this while faced with a severe economic blockade by the USA, making some basic goods hard to find in the shops. Despite the blockade, its health-care programmes, high literacy rates and low crime rates make it a model country for tackling poverty.

For the last few years members of our church have attended the annual demonstration outside the US embassy demanding the release of the Miami Five. These Cubans travelled to Miami to spy on terrorist organizations that plan and commit attacks on Cuban soil. They were arrested and accused of spying against the United States, and have been serving long prison sentences while being denied access to their wives and children. They are victims of the US government's longstanding hatred of the 'threat of a good example', of a system of socialism that has delivered equality, eradicated illiteracy, ended hunger, and proved that 'another world is possible'.

Venezuela

The Venezuelan government of Hugo Chavez has also made impressive efforts to eradicate poverty and to reduce major inequalities within its society. José, a Venezuelan student who stayed at Desmond Tutu House, was originally from a poor barrio near Caracas. 'Before the Bolivarian Revolution', José told us, 'it would never have been possible for someone like me to receive a university education, it was restricted to the wealthy.'

The reforms of Hugo Chavez have caused fierce controversy since he was elected in 1998, especially constitutional changes which have weakened the power of the traditional elites in Venezuela. He has tried to redistribute the wealth flowing from the country's vast oil reserves and nationalize industries crucial to the economy. His policies proved so unpopular with powerful members of the elite that in April 2002 Chavez faced a US-backed coup. The Irish TV documentary *The Revolution Will Not Be Televised* captured the confusion and despair as troops loyal to the Venezuelan elites ousted Chavez. Army Generals, business leaders and even Archbishops were part of the coup, which was immediately endorsed by the US government. But less than two days later, millions of ordinary Venezuelans took to the streets and forced the coup leaders to release Chavez. Since then, Venezuela has moved dramatically ahead with health-care reforms, literacy programmes, large-scale nationalizations and the development of small-scale workers' co-operatives. Despite an almost continuous smear campaign put out by a hostile internal press, largely owned by the previous ruling elites, Chavez and his government have achieved a lot in ten years. To talk about some of those successes, our church invited Charlie Hardy, an ex-Roman Catholic priest who spent many years working in some of the poorest neighbourhoods of the Venezuelan capital. He described the work of the 'Bolivarian circles' that encouraged poor people to improve their education and helped them fight for their rights. His book, *A Cowboy in Caracas*, is an excellent introduction to the history and present situation in Venezuela. He points out that Chavez is one of the few world leaders who talks about the kingdom of God, and whole-heartedly believes that society should play a part in building it.

Christians should show solidarity with countries who try to live out policies that reduce poverty and encourage a life of collectivism and sharing. Solidarity with those who work for the kingdom of God should be a natural starting point for us.

Zimbabwe

The people of Zimbabwe have suffered immeasurably during the tail end of the Mugabe regime. Robert Mugabe may once have been one of the liberators of his country and a great anti-colonial statesman, but his rule has long since become one of corruption and barbarism. In Zimbabwe, once the breadbasket of Africa, 80 per cent of the population is now below the poverty line and the rate of inflation is one of the highest in the world. Mugabe's Zanu PF government were eventually forced to enter in to a unity government with the Movement for Democratic Change (MDC) after the international community condemned the undemocratic elections in March 2008. MDC Leader Morgan Tsvangirai then became a lame duck Prime Minister while President Mugabe retained most of the power over the military and primary state mechanisms. Even when Morgan Tsvangi-rai invited the UN's adviser on torture to see what was happening in

2009, Mugabe had him deported upon arrival at the capital's airport. Thousands have died at the hands of the regime, and tens of thousands have had to flee their homeland.

I first encountered Zimbabweans fleeing the violence of their homeland in Holmewood, Bradford. They were living in exile and also facing racism and prejudice in their new surroundings. Responding to the needs of our Zimbabwean neighbours, St Christopher's parish church hosted a support group for them which, in time, turned into a campaigning group for all of the Zimbabweans in Bradford.

When my ministry moved to the city centre, the Zimbabwean community began meeting in Desmond Tutu House. We launched the Bradford branch of the Movement for Democratic Change (MDC) which the national leadership in exile came to inaugurate. We also hosted a series of national forums to discuss the role of 'civil society' in rebuilding Zimbabwe 'post Mugabe'. Delegates were particularly keen to meet in a house named after Desmond Tutu, one of Africa's strongest critics of Mugabe.

When news emerged of Mugabe's destruction of whole neighbourhoods connected to the opposition in 2007, we decided to hold a service at the cathedral, followed by a march to the city centre. We initially applied to hold a rally in Centenary Square and were told that we would need two million pounds worth of public liability insurance, a bureaucratic obstacle designed to make political protest almost impossible in the city centre. We decided to go ahead and simply petition in the streets instead. As we waited for the service to begin in the cathedral, several police officers arrived, and I was summoned outside. 'We have reason to believe that you are trying to hold an unlawful demonstration in the city centre' said one of the officers. 'We are here to ask you not to march into the city centre, or you may be arrested.' I invited them to come into the service, and explained that it would be hard to stop these women and children from walking into the city centre and sharing what was happening in their home land.

During the sermon, I launched into an attack on the way that Zimbabweans had lost fundamental human rights at home and how they were also beginning to lose them in the UK. Zimbabweans had been treated as criminals by the asylum system, and even at this service, the state were denying them their right to protest. 'Shall we walk into the city centre?' I asked the congregation. 'Yes!' they replied unanimously. We sang 'We are marching in the light of God' as we danced and processed past the bewildered police officers. Two officers accompanied us down the hill towards the city centre. As we approached the pedestrian area, we were met with a police riot van and a greater number of officers. We decided to halt and take the opportunity of petitioning and singing in front of the police van. It was a great location and lots of people were queuing up to see what was going on and taking leaflets.

The police presence and the lively singing made us quite a spectacle. Pavements were blocked with spectators and eventually the senior officer came and said to me, 'You cannot remain here; it is becoming a public safety issue.' 'Where would you rather we went?' I asked. 'We're going to move you to Centenary Square.' 'Great,' I replied, 'that is where we had requested to go months ago!' The police herded us to the square, and in an act of maliciousness forced us to the very centre, refusing us even the right to engage with the public who congregated at the edge of the square. After more prayers interceding for an end to oppression in Zimbabwe, we sang and danced around the stern and embarrassed-looking police officers. The whole incident brought church members and the Zimbabwean community close together, and reinforced our common belief in the importance of the right to democratic protest.

International solidarity, the joy of the Church

The prayers and struggles alongside brothers and sisters throughout the world bring God's kingdom clearly into focus. When we weep and cheer with Burmese, Tibetans, Tamils, Iraqis, Colombians, Cubans, Kurdish, Zimbabweans and many thousands of others, the Church truly becomes the body of Christ. Through an active theology of solidarity, we meet with God in the rainbow of humanity. The churches that will survive in the future will be ones who have embraced the 'other', that have picked up those who are stumbling, then found themselves embraced and healed in the relationship that follows. The joy of the Church is that sense of solidarity with all brothers and sisters in faith: atheists in Cuba, Buddhists from Tibet, and Muslims from Burma. This is the solidarity of globalization.

'Listen then if you have ears!': Solidarity with God's people

Education

- Invite speakers to your church from the Cuba Solidarity Campaign, the Venezuela Information Centre, the Free Burma Campaign and the Free Tibet Movement.
- Ask church members to talk about the international connections they might have.
- Research on the internet and in newspapers what is being said about nations you are interested in. Do they give an accurate reflection of reality?
- Watch documentaries such as *Burma VJ* to help spark discussion about international solidarity movements.

Action

- Join international solidarity movements that you feel strongly about.
- Are there actions such as the 'Total Boycott' which you could publicize and take part in?
- Hold vigils and other acts of solidarity on important anniversaries (the invasion of Tibet, the coup in Venezuela).

Reflection

- Hold a prayer time for the victims of repression in places of conflict around the world.
- Consider the political freedoms that you take for granted; what would you be prepared to do to keep them?
- Do you think that capitalism is fair and sustainable? What role do we have in transforming it? What does the Bible have to say about economics?

Sustaining

- Form a link with a church or community group in a country that you want to show solidarity with.
- Make sure solidarity magazines are available to church members when they are published.
- Build links with refugee communities in your region; find out about their home lands.

Chapter 9

Seekers of Sanctuary

One of the most profound ways in which British churches have tried to live out the gospel has come through our relationships with those seeking sanctuary in our midst. In Bradford, we have responded to the needs of those arriving in our city through a body called Bradford Ecumenical Asylum Concern (BEACON) based at the Touchstone Methodist Centre. Through this group and through the weekly 'Friendship Evening' in Desmond Tutu House run by Student Action for Refugees (STAR), our church has enjoyed rich contacts with the vibrant communities that enter our city.

I learnt the importance of how churches could embrace new communities in Sligo, a place where I go for spiritual renewal each year. Sligo is situated on the west coast of Ireland, just below Donegal County. It is a place full of God's wonder, but not just in the beauty of its glens and waterfalls. It is the people of Sligo who have drawn me back for over twenty years. When I first went there I was sleeping rough, scraping an income from selling sketches of megalithic stones and the mountainous landscapes of Benbulben and Knocknarae. Upon arriving in Sligo for the first time, I headed to the Anglican Cathedral. With my long, tangled hair, scruffy beard and the whiff of someone sleeping in abandoned buildings, I was not particularly welcomed. After several attempts, I decided to give the Methodist church a shot. The response could not have been more different. I was immediately taken for Sunday lunch by Marion and Herbie Watts where I was also offered a shower, a sign of the odour I must have been emitting!

Sligo is a small place, and so those arriving from Nigeria, Zimbabwe and Sierra Leone have not gone unnoticed. The Methodist church reacted positively to the new arrivals and set about serving this community in a number of ways. The hostel that housed many of the new arrivals was situated a fair distance from the town centre, and there were no buses. Members of the Methodist church offered lifts to the markets and shopping centres in Sligo. From the friendships made through these acts of hospitality, many of those seeking sanctuary now attend the Methodist church. It is one of the most multicultural places on the west coast on a Sunday. Numbers have doubled, and the church has new life and has found the resources to rebuild its church hall and refurbish its main chapel. Though some in the church have found the transition difficult, many have had their faith reinvigorated. By contrast, the Anglican cathedral nearby has an ageing and diminishing congregation. The message is clear: our churches can reach out to the stranger, and be transformed by the experience. When we shelter those in need, we will grow spiritually. If our churches choose not to do so, then we may wither like a condemned fig-tree.

No borders: opposing an unjust system

The UK immigration service should be something that we are proud of. It ought to be a way of protecting some of the most vulnerable people in the world by ensuring their safety and enabling them to adjust to their new home. Occasionally it does seem to deliver and it is a delight to meet those who are thankful to the British government for all the help and support they have received. One such example is the Mussanzi family from the Congo. Ben and Kongosi Musanzi have worked tirelessly for peace since their acceptance for refugee status in the UK. They have instilled hope in many through their organization, the Centre for Conflict Resolution. They are a powerful testimony to when the system works well, giving safety to those fleeing violence and making the best use of the new talents brought into our community.

For many people though, the experience is not so pleasant. The political climate means that parties vie with each other as to which one is seen to be the toughest on asylum-seekers. The system is unduly harsh and set up in such a way as to act as a deterrent for most people coming into our nation. Asylum-seekers are sometimes treated as potential criminals, and in court they may have to sit in front of a stern judge and a hostile legal representative of the state. They will often have to do this without any legal support of their own, and in a language and culture of which they may have only a limited understanding.

If this is not enough to contend with, the media in general has waged a war against people seeking sanctuary, and has demonized them so much that the general public has an extremely prejudiced idea of who asylum-seekers are and why they have come. Churches have become increasingly aware of the injustices of the system, from the condition of housing stock offered on a 'no choice' basis, to the cruel practice of dawn raids and detention centres for those, including children, who are deemed unsuccessful. Though the coalition government elected in 2010 has promised to end child imprisonment, it has not made this commitment a priority.

Ultimately as Christians, we must ask ourselves what a Christlike response would be to people seeking sanctuary. Jesus himself was sent into exile as a child. Would we like to think of Joseph, Mary and Jesus detained in camps after enduring dawn raids? There are no borders in God's kingdom; it is we who have created them. As a nation bestowed with abundance, we in the UK should learn to share our gifts with those who come from less fortunate situations. People of faith must learn to live without borders if they wish to transcend the rule of people and choose instead to live within the reign of God.

State child abuse: dawn raids and detention

It was the Tuesday of Holy Week when I was awakened by a telephone call just after 6 a.m.: 'They have come for Margaret and Paul, hurry, please come now!' a distraught voice pleaded between sobs of tears. I got dressed quickly, jumped on my bicycle and raced towards their home.

Margaret had suffered horrendous abuse in her home country before fleeing for her life with her children. Following the death of her husband, she had been repeatedly gang-raped and infected with HIV. She had been advised to claim status in the UK under health grounds but had lost her case. Based on fresh evidence, however, a new claim had been made through the Home Office. The fresh claim should have meant that she did not have to worry about dawn raids;

but there I was, hurtling down the road on my bike, clutching in my hand a copy of her recently submitted fresh claim, determined to stop her deportation.

Two unmarked detention vans were parked outside. I ran up the steps and knocked on the door. A police officer opened the front door slightly, just revealing his face. 'Please allow me to come into Margaret's house, I'm her priest, and I have evidence as to why this is an illegal removal.' The police officer shut the door and didn't return until I pounded on the door again. 'You can't come in,' he explained; 'removal proceedings are taking place.' I jammed my foot in the door and said: 'I have come to pray with a member of my congregation, and you will not stop me. I demand to see the officer in charge.' Eventually I was allowed in.

Paul, Margaret's son, was sitting on the sofa in the front room. He wiped away a tear, and tried to smile. 'Pastor, thank you for coming, let me make you a cup of tea.' He stood up, but an immigration officer stepped forward and pushed him violently back into the seat. 'Do not move!' he shouted aggressively. I tried to defuse the hostile situation: 'Let me make the tea!' I stepped into the kitchen. 'Who else would like a drink? I'll just make this while someone gets the senior officer, is that all right?'

A few minutes later a tough-looking female immigration officer came down the stairs, followed by Margaret flanked by two other officers. Margaret was numb, silent, subdued. 'How can I help you?' asked the senior officer.

'I have a letter showing that a fresh claim has recently been placed with the Home Office,' I replied. 'If you look at this, we might be able to save everybody a wasted journey.' She looked at the letter. 'I still have orders that need to be carried through, I'm sorry; I can't change the proceedings now.' I continued to protest: 'Paul needs to get to school, the last time you guys made this mistake, he missed nearly a week off school while the mess got sorted out.' This was the second time this family had undergone a dawn raid. After the first raid, Paul was so frightened that he couldn't sleep at night even when they were eventually released back to their home in Bradford. Until the fresh claim had gone in, his mum would try to reassure him by going out each morning at 5 a.m. to keep watch for the immigration vans.

'I'll give you the number of the senior immigration official at Waterside,' the female officer spoke apologetically. 'Maybe it can be dealt with before the family is sent down to Yarl's Wood.' Margaret began to sob. The name of the detention centre is enough to evoke fear in all mothers, knowing it is a terrible place for children to be incarcerated in.

I sat beside Margaret and asked her if she would like me to pray with her. She nodded through the tears, and I held her hand in one hand and Paul's in another. 'Lord we pray for your mercy on this loving family, who have suffered so much. We pray that you will protect them through whatever is to happen next and that they will always be aware of your presence with them. And Lord, we ask for your forgiveness on the officers here, committing an unlawful detention of an innocent family,' (lots of uncomfortable shuffling around us) 'and we pray that they will do their duties respectfully and with compassion. Father, we give thanks for Margaret and Paul, and all the love they have shown this community, be with them always, Amen.' Having prayed this prayer I was asked to leave, and the family were escorted out. 'I'll get on to the solicitors straight away,' I said to Margaret as she was led away.

As Margaret was getting into the van, Andrew, Bobbi and Phil arrived, members of Student Action for Refugees (STAR). I had almost forgotten I had called them while getting dressed. Phil took photos, which proved helpful for media coverage later. As the vans drove away we were left with an awful feeling that we may never see the family again.

I spoke to the immigration service at the Waterside Centre in Leeds and was promised that the matter would be looked into, and that as a special concession, Margaret and Paul would be kept in Leeds and not taken to Yarl's Wood until our solicitors had had a chance to speak to them. This turned out to be a complete lie. By the time Margaret's solicitors contacted Waterside at 8 a.m., the family had been whisked off on the 150-mile journey south. The immigration service told Margaret's solicitors that the family were due to be flown home on Tuesday, the day after Easter Bank Holiday. It would make it almost impossible for the solicitors to act over the Easter break.

On Good Friday the Home Office rang me to say that a mistake had been made. They admitted losing the fresh claim submitted by the solicitors for the family a few months before. However, Margaret was not released. Instead, the immigration service held an emergency hearing to discuss her fresh claim. This was done in secret, without Margaret's solicitors present to argue her case. There was no opportunity to appeal the decision made nor to submit further evidence. My last telephone conversation with Margaret was on Easter Sunday. It was hard to share the joy of the resurrection, the victory of love over the powers of evil, while Margaret faced immediate deportation. Paul was unable to stop crying. Margaret was trying to keep his spirits up, but Paul, with an English education since he was eight, and about to start his GCSEs, knew he was about to lose everything he had ever known. His promising football career was in tatters.

Margaret and Paul were deported on the Tuesday and went to stay with a relative on the outskirts of Nairobi. There were nine of them living in a single room. Paul was spending his time curled up in the corner of the room, tearful and refusing to eat. Having lost friends, education and his hopes, he felt like he had lost his whole world. Margaret managed to give me a call: 'I don't know what to do. I think Paul's suicidal.'

I assured her we would do all that we could even though they were out of the country. I organized a meeting with Laura O'Connor and Judy Midgely, members of Bradford Ecumenical Concern, Andrew, Maya and others from Student Action for Refugees. We decided to contact Paul's school, as they had no idea what had happened to him. Laura and I met with the headteacher and Paul's tutor. They were shocked; it was a close-knit Catholic school where Paul had been a star pupil, both academically and on the football field. Most of the staff, however, had no idea that he was from a family seeking asylum. We decided that Laura and I would do a special assembly for Paul's year group. His friends deserved to know what had happened to him.

A week later, 150 fourteen- and fifteen-year-olds were assembled in the school hall. It was a predominantly white working-class school in a poor part of Leeds. It was hard to predict how these kids would react. First, we asked pupils to fill in a questionnaire about asylum-seeker issues. Their answers revealed the general media myths:

asylum-seekers got better houses, received good benefits and were mostly here for financial reasons. We slowly explained that the amount of money asylum-seekers receive each week is only 70 per cent of basic income support; that they are often housed in the worst housing stock that nobody else would accept; and that they are not economic migrants but come from war zones and areas of human-rights violations. Despite our best efforts, however, the youngsters were noisy and argumentative, refusing to take the assembly seriously.

Then I began to talk about Paul. He was a popular kid, everyone knew him and nobody understood why he had just disappeared after the Easter break. As I began to tell the story of the dawn raid, the room went silent. When I got to the part of him trying to get up to make me a cup of tea but being pushed back in his chair, friends of his broke down in tears. They were devastated. I will never forget watching some of those fifteen-year-old lads being unable to stop themselves from crying, unable to comprehend what they were hearing. Their close friend was gone, probably for good.

A few days later the headteacher contacted me. The staff and pupils had decided to pay for Paul to continue his education in Africa. They had already contacted a Catholic school in the country's capital, and fees had been arranged. The young people had decided to fund-raise so that Paul would be able to do his A-levels afterwards. Our church contributed money for textbooks and a uniform, and life became a little bit more bearable for Margaret and Paul. They email me regularly to let me know how things are going. Life is hard and they are still in hiding, making it complicated for Margaret to find work. But school life has made such a difference, and Paul is making the most of his opportunity. He is even playing in a football team again.

A matter of life and death: Sara's story

Sara and her children began coming to our church after attending one of our friendship evenings at Desmond Tutu House. Most of her family had been killed in a dispute over land in the Philippines. A company with powerful connections was buying up land in an area where European mining operations were due to expand. Those who did not accept the paltry sums being offered were subject to brutal intimidation. Sara's husband Luis did not want to sell and soon suffered the consequences: his parents were murdered. Sara, Luis and their two children were forced to flee to an uncle's house. A few months later the uncle too was murdered. Sara and Luis left straight away, with their two young children, and headed for the anonymity of the capital city of Manila.

One day Sara was coming back from taking her eldest daughter to a nearby school and found the house surrounded by police officers. Luis and their one-year-old daughter had both been shot through the head. In Filipino land disputes, children are commonly killed in order to prevent them later claiming the family land back, or from taking revenge. After this horrific event, Sara realized that to have a chance of protecting her eldest daughter, Anna, she must flee the country. A local priest hid them in his home before buying tickets for a flight to the UK.

By the time we met them, Sara had been in the country for over a year and Anna was doing really well at school. Sara's appeal for asylum had failed, however, and she was becoming increasingly worried that she might be sent back to the Philippines. 'I am frightened of staying at my house at night time,' she explained to me. The Home Office had rejected her claim because they said she was lying about her husband's murder. There was a further complication. Sara was pregnant. A man had befriended her and said that he could help her. He turned up one day saying that he had nowhere to live and insisted that he move into her flat. She became pregnant, and when she told him, he disappeared overnight.

At the friendship evening we began helping Sara to gain new evidence about her case so that a fresh claim could be made should her appeal fail. We organized the translation of the death certificates of her murdered husband and child. I also tracked down the priest in the Philippines who had taken them into his house. This had been a difficult task because the priest himself had gone into hiding after helping Sara and her family escape from the gang. Shortly after Sara had left, the gang kidnapped the priest's eldest son. He was tortured, then released when the gang realized that Sara was no longer in the country. The priest and his family decided to move.

Despite evidence from human-rights organizations, the British government believes that the Philippines is safe and generally refuses asylum cases from the country. Nevertheless the judicial and police system in the Philippines consistently fail to protect people such as Sara.

Our church felt that we had to help Sara in any way we could. She was terrified of dawn raids, so we arranged for people to stay at her house each night. They reassured her and would be at hand to help resist any attempt to deport her. We put in place a 'phone tree' so that one call would lead to many of us arriving to physically block any detention. We also ensured that Sara obtained a letter from her midwife indicating the stage of her pregnancy, so that she could prove that it was illegal to forcibly remove her. The letter turned out to be a Godsend. When eight immigration officials turned up at 11 p.m. one night, they initially refused to believe she was heavily pregnant and started bagging up her belongings. The student who was staying the night remembered the letter and insisted that the senior officer read it. The officer made some phone calls and then they withdrew. A few days later Sara received a letter saying that her asylum claim had been refused. She was to inform an official when the child was born, after which she was to be deported when the baby was a month old.

We worked hard to get a new claim in. We sought advice from the Immigration Advisory Service who give free legal support to a limited number of asylum-seekers. Her case worker believed the best way forward was for Sara to have a full psychiatric assessment for the trauma she had gone through, and for a claim to be made on 'humanitarian' grounds. The trouble was that there was a long waiting list for such professional advice, and there was a risk it would take much longer than the few months we had. A letter was sent to the Home Office asking for more time while this medical assessment was being sought, and we had a copy of this letter at Sara's house to try to stave off another raid.

While we waited, there were many joys for the team of churchgoers and students who were helping with the case. Tansy and Ben from SoulSpace looked after Anna while Sara went to hospital to have her child. Jenifer, from STAR, supported Sara through the birth itself.

Two weeks later Sara insisted on a baptism service during SoulSpace, and Gabriella was welcomed into the church community. At the service we vowed to do all we could to protect this little one and the rest of her family. That vow was soon to be put into practice. One day Sara came back home from shopping to discover that someone had been in her flat. She called me and asked me to ring her housing providers to see if they had visited. I rang them up, but they refused to discuss the matter with me. Later that afternoon, while playing with her toys, Anna discovered a letter and took it to her mother. The letter was a notification of a warrant which allowed UKBA to return any time in the following nine days. We had to get them out of there fast.

We found a spare room in a nearby student house and arranged a rota for getting Anna to school. We had to buy enough time for the psychiatric assessment to be done. A few days later, Sara got a phone call from school. The police had come and asked to see Anna. Her class tutor refused to allow her to go as they didn't have Sara's permission for anyone else to collect Anna from school. The police waited outside until home time, but the headteacher had Anna taken out by the back entrance.

It was a race against time. We mounted a media campaign to argue Sara's case and got front-page headlines in the regional press. This forced the local MP to take the matter seriously and get involved in the case. He got agreement that the immigration department would allow time for the psychiatric assessment to be completed. Until this process had been finished they would not try to detain or remove Sara and her children. Consequently Sara, Anna and Gabriella were able to move back safely into their flat and Anna could go back to school as normal.

A year later, despite all our efforts, Sara lost her case. She could not face going into hiding with her children again and so in the end she allowed herself to be 'voluntarily' repatriated. Back in the Philippines, Sara, Anna and Gabriella were forced to go into hiding, and Anna, who had been one of the brightest pupils in her class, is no longer able to go to school.

These matters of social justice cannot be dealt with by our churches in a half-hearted way. These are not theoretical discussions but are matters of life and death. Churches can make huge differences if they are well organized and prepared to take risks on the side of such vulnerable people. Even when we cannot prevent the eventual deportation of families, the fact that we tried has powerful repercussions for both our lives and the lives of those we seek to help.

A city of sanctuary

As well as supporting individual families that drift into our churches, liberation theology demands that we attempt to tackle such issues in a more structural way. An important national project that does this is the 'City of Sanctuary' movement. It began in Sheffield with the support of many churches and community groups and is headed by Inderjit Boghal, a former president of the Methodist Conference.

The work of City of Sanctuary is fundamentally concerned with challenging the public perception of those entering the UK for sanctuary. The term 'seeking sanctuary' is preferred over the negative connotations associated with 'asylum'. The notion of sanctuary gives dignity to those seeking it, while encompassing ideals such as hospitality and safety. The idea of sanctuary conveys a sense of the responsibility of the hosts to protect and to welcome, and the City of Sanctuary movement envisages that towns and cities restate this obligation to those who have fled persecution elsewhere. The way each city does this varies from area to area, but fundamentally City of Sanctuary hopes to get public, voluntary and private bodies and organizations to sign up to a statement of support for the movement, recognizing the contribution that those seeking sanctuary make to our society. Any organization joining the movement can publicly display a symbol which helps sanctuary seekers feel welcomed, knowing that the shop or service understands their particular hardships.

In Bradford, we wanted to give a voice to our new arrivals, to hear their stories first-hand, and so we decided to hold a series of public meetings entitled 'Stories of Sanctuary'. We invited participants to share their own histories of struggle along with the stories of the voluntary organizations that support them. The meetings gave us a chance to celebrate people's lives, and bring together diverse groups.

Those seeking sanctuary are liberated by the whole process;

instead of being seen as a nuisance, they are valued. Instead of being isolated by their experience, the stories help them realize they are not alone. When one person tells their story, they are reassured to hear: 'That happened to me also: we too were made to feel like criminals'. Such story-telling events bring together our common humanity. Women from the Congo and Colombia recognize similar experiences of rape and being marginalized. Men finally admit to each other the fear they experienced in the torture chamber. People of all faiths openly tell of the way that God walked with them in their struggle. After the stories, a shared meal, listening to music and dancing together, everyone is changed for ever, and for some, healing can finally begin.

More recently, City of Sanctuary has tried to pull together a 'manifesto' that envisages what a place of safety would actually look and feel like. The essentials are fundamental human rights such as: the right to work, the right to a decent education, the right to good housing without fear of being moved around (many seekers of sanctuary are provided housing on a 'no choice' basis which means that they can be rehoused in a different city with sometimes only a few days' notice). The City of Sanctuary movement believes that no one should live in fear. No child should experience a dawn raid in the UK. All sanctuary seekers should have access to a solicitor who can ensure that they have a fair hearing. Many churches involved with the movement have offered schemes to swap vouchers for cash so that sanctuary seekers could have some dignity and choice in their personal finances.

The rights of sanctuary seekers are important, but a culture of hospitality is also essential. It is a fundamental principle in Christianity that we seek the face of Christ in all those who we meet. From the story of the sheep and the goats (Matthew 25), we know that we encounter Jesus in the most vulnerable. When Jesus talks about entering the kingdom of heaven, he points out that it is our treatment of others that provides the key. Theologian Joan Chittister describes hospitality as our ability to bring people to God 'one mind at a time'. Quite rightly, the City of Sanctuary movement believes that hospitality should be at the heart of our churches and institutions.

Care and hospitality at Thornbury

The Bradford suburb of Thornbury houses one of the ten tribunal courts for those seeking refugee status. Each morning people from all over the region make their way to the building for 10 a.m. When the courts were first opened, very little provision was made for those attending. Defendants are encouraged not to bring young children but few families had any alternative. Only a coin-operated coffee machine and a chocolate-bar dispenser were offered by way of refreshment – little use to those who were given their allowance in the form of a voucher. After attending court with several sanctuary seekers, a group of us decided to challenge this lack of hospitality.

Local churches decided to hold a protest asking for better facilities for visitors. We had a letter which we decided to present one morning while the court was in session. Judy Midgley and Geoff Reid would provide boxes of fruit to be given to all entering the building as a sign of hospitality. On the morning of the protest, several refugees, three 'dog-collars', two nuns and assorted members of Bradford's samba band handed out apples and bananas while waiting for a representative from the courts to accept the letter. The police arrived shortly after the drums began to beat and we were asked to move to the other side of the road so that we did not disturb the courts.

'We also must ask you to desist from handing over fruit to anyone entering the premises,' one of the policemen said sternly. The samba band being moved on I could understand – we were not playing our best, and our best was never that good – but why not hand out apples? 'Why can't we hand out fruit?' I asked. 'You might have poisoned them,' the policemen said, then looked at the nuns, and seemed to realize how ridiculous he sounded and added apologetically: 'It's a health and safety issue.' The centre manager then came out but refused to accept the letter. 'It must be sent through official channels to our head office,' she explained. It seemed that even protesters were not immune to the mad bureaucracy of the asylum system.

A few days after the protest hit the headlines, I got a call from the centre manager we had met at the court entrance. 'You're absolutely right,' she said, 'the provision for people coming here is awful, but I'm trying my best to improve things. Can we meet?' A few weeks later I found myself inside the courts explaining our idea to open the Methodist church across the street as a base for hospitality. The manager liked the plan and couldn't have been more helpful in supporting its implementation.

As the months passed, the project, Care and Hospitality at Thornbury (CHAT) was developed by the Revd Rita Armitage, Joe Batt, Heather Grinter, Kath Larrard and a host of wonderful people from the local Methodist church. Most people were too afraid to leave the court building, so the staff at the centre provided us with an old trolley, and let us provide refreshments inside the court waiting-rooms. The system worked extremely well, and we were warmly welcomed by the court users and staff alike.

Six months into the project I was invited to give a talk at a Home Office conference in London for chaplaincy teams operating in the court system. I had been asked to come along as Bradford was the first immigration tribunal court to have a hospitality programme and it was by now being talked about as a 'national model'. A few weeks later, the centre manager rang with a shaky voice, 'I need you to come in for a meeting as soon as possible.' When we met she explained that someone from the Home Office had come up from London and told them that the project must close. At first the man from the Home Office argued about the danger of 'proselytism', but the centre manager explained that she took part in our volunteer training, and that she was sure that our volunteers behaved professionally. CHAT even had several volunteers from other faith traditions.

Then the real problem emerged. The Home Office visitor revealed a large folder containing details about me. The senior judge at the court and the centre manager were shown pictures of me being arrested at demonstrations, from Menwith Hill spy base to Faslane nuclear centre. Clippings of campaigns I had been involved with were carefully marked with a yellow highlighter by a conscientious Home Office worker. The response of the staff was deeply heartening. The Home Office visitor was reminded that the courts were run by the tribunal service, an independent body. They refused to close the project and CHAT continued to carry out its work. It was a fascinating insight into the workings of the Home Office. Fortunately the relationships of trust we had built up had managed to save the project.

William's story

I met William at the Refugee Council in Leeds. He had arrived in London that day but the immigration service had sent him to Leeds where he was then told he must report to a centre in Liverpool the next day, but in the meantime he had nowhere to stay. I overheard staff at the Refugee Council agonizing about what to do, so I stepped in. He had no English, and I have no French, but despite this I took him home to Bradford, otherwise he would have spent the night at Leeds station. Once home I rang Judy, a friend who could speak French, and she joined us for a meal.

Over the meal William began to tell his story. He had been beaten and tortured in a Congolese jail for being part of an opposition party. While William was in prison his brother was murdered by government forces. The local village priest was convinced William would be next and took the four-day journey to the prison where he bribed an official to obtain William's release. The priest gave William photos of his brother's open coffin, deliberately left open so that the people could see the torture inflicted by the authorities. The priest arranged a flight, first to Cape Town, then to Heathrow.

After the meal, William showed us these photos of his brother and wept. To demonstrate the brutality of his torturers he took off his shirt and we saw the scars on his back. He was anxious to know if his family was safe and we offered him a phone so he could call his wife. He managed to get through and more tears came, but this time they were tears of joy. The village priest had not yet returned and his wife thought that he was already dead. After the call we all hugged each other and he asked us to pray with him. He prayed with passion, thanking God and offering himself to the Lord. After he had thanked us thoroughly he went to his room, where we heard him pray throughout the night. After a breakfast full of smiles and broken French, I took him to the station. A few months later I received a phone call from someone sharing a hostel with him. He wanted us to know that he was doing well, and he was grateful for that first night in England and the hospitality our family had shown. I told him that it was us who were grateful; it had been a real blessing to meet him and to witness such faith.

I was fortunate enough to hear Jean Vanier speak when he came to Leeds in 2007. The French priest and founder of the L'Arche community spoke gently about the story of the good Samaritan (Luke 10.25–37). Vanier placed emphasis on the time that the Samaritan spent with someone who was suffering – how the Samaritan assessed the needs of the injured man before doing what was needed: bathing his wounds then treating them with oil and wine. The Samaritan gave up his own comforts including his horse, taking the man to a place of safety. The Samaritan probably even spent the entire night nursing the man's broken body. He made sure that the man's needs were dealt with by the innkeeper, promising to make sure that the cost would be met when he returned. Jean Vanier focused on the compassion of the Samaritan and the time taken up by his care for the injured man.

The more we open our homes and our churches to those seeking sanctuary, the more time we spend with them, the more we will be blessed. Even simple acts of hospitality can mean a great deal to those who have gone through so much.

'Listen then if you have ears!': Commitment to sanctuary

Education

- Find out about the groups and services provided locally for those seeking sanctuary.
- Invite someone from a refugee forum or other such body that represents those seeking sanctuary to a church meeting.
- Collect a sample of stories about sanctuary seekers from a range of newspapers over one week, then discuss them in a group.
- Check out websites of groups like the Refugee Council, share one thing you didn't know with others in your church community.
- Go along to a 'Stories of Sanctuary' night by a nearby City of Sanctuary group.

114 A Just Church

Act

- Volunteer at language conversation classes.
- Write to your local MP about the right to work campaign. This means that sanctuary seekers should be able to earn a living while their case is being heard.
- Get involved with your local STAR or 'No Borders' group.
- Join Church Action on Poverty's 'Living Ghosts' campaign which highlights those who live with no access to benefits and housing. Take up the challenge to live on Red Cross food parcels/vouchers for a week.
- Find out if church members can go on 'Mckenzie friends' training to help sanctuary seekers without legal support.

Reflection

- If you attempted to live as a 'Living Ghost', keep a journal of the experience. Share the experiences with your community.
- In a group, discuss the impact of going to court, awaiting decisions, worrying about dawn raids, being detained. What would a 'Christian' immigration policy look like?
- Hold a reflective service for the regions of the world where people are forced to flee persecution.
- What impact have your experiences of befriending sanctuary seekers had on your faith?

Sustaining

- Could your church host a drop-in service for refugees and those seeking sanctuary? How would you run such a scheme?
- Think about how you include seekers of sanctuary in your church community.
- Affiliate your church with local and national groups that are concerned with the welfare of sanctuary seekers. Send delegates to regional conferences or training events.
- If your city does not have a 'City of Sanctuary' group, why not have a meeting with other local churches and consider setting one up?

Chapter 10

Make Poverty History

The story of the rich man and Lazarus (Luke 16.19–31) is one of the most demanding parables in the Bible. Luke tells us about a man who fails to respond to the needs of Lazarus, a poor man who is hungry and lies at his gate. The tale then says how Lazarus dies and goes to heaven while the rich man dies and goes to torment. In hell the rich man begs Abraham to send Lazarus with his finger dipped in water to cool his tongue. Abraham explains that it is impossible, for there is a great chasm that has been fixed to prevent crossing from one side to another. The rich man then pleads for someone from the land of the dead to go and warn his family, but Abraham says that if they failed to listen to Moses and the Prophets, then 'they will not be convinced even if someone rises from the grave'.

God gives it a go anyway. Jesus does indeed rise from the grave, but it turns out that Abraham was right: the rich are still reluctant to change their ways. Each day in this world of super abundance, up to 30,000 children die of poverty-related hunger and disease. Even in Britain and the USA where there is the greatest wealth ever created in history, there are people struggling to feed and clothe their children and who cannot afford their winter fuel bills. Both at home and abroad, the gap between the rich and poor is widening, and with the effects of climate change looming, it looks like the chasm will continue to grow. Thankfully, the work of Christian Aid, CAFOD, Church Action on Poverty and a plethora of faith-based anti-poverty groups has helped churches to focus on the issues. It would be helpful for all emerging Churches to link themselves to both international and local anti-poverty campaigns. JustChurch has benefited from the active support of Christian Aid, and they have helped us to keep issues of greed and poverty at the heart of our thinking and doing.

A world of debt

Indebtedness is at the heart of global inequality. In the prayer that Jesus taught us to use (Matthew 6.9–14) we are invited to dwell on two important aspects of poverty: first, the need to have enough food for everyone to live on ('Give us each day the bread we need'); and second, to change the way we deal with the ownership of land, wealth and resources ('Forgive us our debts, as we forgive those who are in debt to us').

The Lloyds and Midland boycott and the Jubilee 2000 campaign brought the issue of international debt into the public arena. Tens of thousands marched to Birmingham in 1998, and in 2005 hundreds of thousands flocked to Edinburgh for the G8 summit, but still the combination of international debt and trading inequalities means that the poorest nations have little chance of escaping the cycle of poverty. In the case of Haiti and Pakistan, it took catastrophic earthquakes or flooding to persuade rich nations to take debt relief seriously.

Debt is not only a third world phenomenon. In Britain, housing estates suffer from unscrupulous loan sharks who keep people in a perpetual cycle of debt. Bradford is home to one of the largest of the 'legitimate' loan sharks, Provident Financial, known as 'The Provi'. On the estates and in the advice centres of Bradford, the problems associated with having 'The Provi' come to your door are well known. The Provi is Britain's leading doorstep lender, calling on houses in the poorest parts of the nation and offering loans to people who cannot get them through the high street banking system. Provident Financial believe that they are the 'friend to the poor', giving loans to those without access to normal financial services. Yet no friend charges 179% APR. For every £100 borrowed, £180 will be expected back. The Provident are, however, just one of the many legal moneylenders who benefit from the government's failure to put a cap on the interest rates companies can charge. Until a cap is put in place, then companies will continue to take what they can from the poorest of the poor.

The poverty of the Christian response

Provident Financial has an interesting effect on Bradford's local politicians and the city's churches. MPs and local councillors do not want to speak out against one of the most successful companies in the city; it is a large employer, and in 2010 opened its brand-new offices in the heart of the city centre. Local churches are hesitant to criticize such a prominent business, partly because it is a generous giver of funds and resources. Provident Financial is surprisingly linked to another big Bradford employer, Christians Against Poverty (CAP), an organization offering debt advice. The Provident boasts on its website that it has been involved with CAP since its inception, and it has certainly been a generous sponsor. In turn, CAP refuses to condemn the Provident's lending practices and on its website even gives advice on how to best pay back a loan from the 'Provi'. This may not be too surprising when you consider that the founder of Christians Against Poverty, Andy Kirkby, used to work for the financial lending sector. CAP do good work in helping those in debt, and have many excellent debt advisers, but they fail to see the dangers of being too close to one of the major sources of debt in the UK.

To coincide with one of the Provident's Annual General Meetings, members from our church and several debt workers from advice centres decided to do our own 'door-stepping'. We began outside the city-centre branch of BrightHouse, a company which sells furniture and electrical goods to people with a low credit rating. Customers pay for goods in small weekly instalments, but interest rates are so high that they end up paying a small fortune. In response to this, we decided to hand out leaflets telling passers-by about the scandalous tactics of companies like BrightHouse. It was also a good excuse to get out the samba drums once again. After a while the police were called, not by the BrightHouse staff but by someone from a neighbouring shop. She came out to tell me she was a prominent member of a local Anglican church and had opposed my appointment. Seeing what we were doing, she apparently now 'had proof that our little fresh expression was a dangerous waste of money'!

The samba band weaved through the city and arrived outside the offices of Provident Financial. We leafleted the people going in and then I went into the foyer and asked to meet with a member of the management. After I was ejected we kept on playing and it was not long before someone came out to 'begin discussions' with us. If we stopped drumming, they might allow a meeting with executives from the company at a later date. I said that we would stop the protest when someone from senior management listened to our concerns face to face. Our drumming eventually won out and before we left I had met with three senior members of staff in their swish fifth-floor offices. Even at this height, the noise from the samba band outside was particularly awful. If we had carried on drumming for a few days, I'm sure that even the chief executive, Peter Crook, would have agreed to national caps on interest rates.

We decided to have a longer conversation in a few weeks' time. This allowed me the chance to invite along Alan Thornton from Church Action on Poverty (an organization with a very distinct ethos and outlook from Christians Against Poverty). Church Action on Poverty had been a serious thorn in the side of the Provident, initiating high-level government meetings calling for a cap on the interest rates that the loan companies were able to charge. Consequently Provident Financial had taken an unusual interest in the activities of Church Action on Poverty. Under freedom of information legislation, Alan Thornton had discovered that the company kept extensive records of his actions and those of the national director of Church Action on Poverty, Niall Cooper.

Sitting in the offices of Provident Financial a few weeks later, Alan did a great job of trying to convince the organization as to why it should join the campaign for a cap on interest rates; it would actually be good for them, helping to curb the activities of less scrupulous companies and thus eliminating much of the company's opposition. However, the management was more concerned about arguing that the 'Provi' was 'the true friend of the poor', lending where nobody else would and citing the company's extensive financial giving to Church-based organizations, especially the work of Christians Against Poverty. They said that they were deeply hurt that a member of the clergy and a Church-based organization were so actively campaigning against their business.

The way liberation theology responds to such issues is illustrated by the difference of approaches between Christians Against Poverty and Church Action on Poverty. Jim Wallis from the Sojourners movement says, 'Christians are often good at pulling people out of the river when they are drowning, but not so good at going upstream and finding out who is pushing them in.' Christians Against Poverty may well be good at pulling people out who are drowning in their own debt problems, but Church Action on Poverty goes upstream to challenge those who are causing the problem. Christians Against Poverty works on an individual basis, one case study at a time, whereas Church Action on Poverty deals with the structural causes of those problems. In the Gospel stories, Jesus is moved to acts of compassion towards individuals, but he also trains his disciples to look at the causes of sin and is ultimately prepared to 'go upstream' to Jerusalem, to the root of the problem and face those responsible. This is what a liberating theology demands of us.

According to Joel Bakan's book *The Corporation*, many large organizations are incapable of making good moral decisions because they are designed to make as much profit for the shareholder as possible. To deflect attention from the often immoral actions of their companies, they must project the image of being socially caring. 'Corporate Social Responsibility' programmes and policies are common in even the most odious of companies. Individual members of staff eventually believe their own propaganda. Provident Financial actually believes it is a friend to the poor. BP staff believe that they are helping the environment. Bankers with huge bonuses believe that they are creating wealth through the trickle-down effect. Churches must shatter these delusions and support stronger regulation of these companies. Corporations inevitably put profit before people. Liberation theology demands that the needs of people and planet must always take priority.

Defending the 'market': taking on Morrisons

Taking on the 'powers that be' is a daunting undertaking and many ministers feel ill prepared for the task. Theological colleges have tried to address this problem, and some, such as Queen's in Birmingham, have recently experimented in 'prophetic ministry' courses. John Hull and others at Queen's are determined that all students are exposed to acts of prophetic justice as an essential part of their studies. I had begun my own journey of tackling large corporations with the Nestlé boycott campaign at Bradford University. The University had bestowed an honorary degree on the chair of Nestlé UK and our protests resulted in face-to-face discussions with senior members of the company. Despite the deaths of thousands of babies due to irresponsible marketing of the baby milk powder they sold, Nestlé were not interested in changing such a profitable policy.

Taking on vast multinational companies and government policy is demanding, time consuming, and sometimes demoralizing. But with even a small amount of faith, mountains can be moved. I want to illustrate this with a story of a small group of people trying to change the policy of a giant of a company.

The supermarket chain Morrisons announced that they were to close their store in central Bradford. It was a medium-sized outlet, and they wanted to concentrate on large, out-of-town developments. The store was attached to the city-centre market and was a vital lifeline for those on low incomes in the city. For those without a car – the elderly, students, refugees, those on relatively poor incomes – this supermarket was the only place to shop. Being close to the market, you could also buy a wide range of items cheaply. The market traders were fearful that if the supermarket closed, many small shops might have to close down. These small businesses were vital to local employment, and offered a chance for locally produced goods such as meat and vegetables to be sold. The market needed defending, and that meant making Morrisons keep its store open.

JustChurch members organized and helped collect signatures on a petition. Market stallholders got involved, as did volunteers from 'Global Exchange', and we soon had over 4,000 names in just a few days. There were queues of people eager to sign, even supermarket staff members popped out during their lunch breaks to sign, concerned about their jobs. Günter and other market stallholders circulated the petition. The manager of Bradford Community Broadcasting (BCB) Mary Dowson became heavily involved and helped get others active in the campaign. Armed with the petition and a local press photographer, Mary and I turned up at Morrisons new corporate offices in Thornbury. The security staff refused to accept the petition and eventually turned us away. The photograph in the local newspaper showed a dejected priest and a sad-faced Mrs Dowson grimly holding up the petition that the company had refused even to accept. It was a public relations disaster for Morrisons. I soon received a phone call and an apology: 'There was a terrible mix-up and a confusion as to what the petition was about, Reverend Howson,' came the apologetic voice on the phone. 'We will arrange to meet with you and Mary as soon as convenient for you both.'

Morrisons new offices were very impressive, and we felt a little awed as we waited to meet a senior executive, a cousin of Mr Morrison. We handed over the petition and explained our concerns. In turn, the executive explained the new corporate strategy and stated that the city-centre shop was uneconomic. Even though the company had begun in the marketplace nearby, the shop had to go. With no movement from the company, we asked for a second meeting, in which we hinted that some in our campaign group had reluctantly considered organizing a boycott. The *Telegraph & Argus* posted a picture of me holding a sign that said, 'Remember your roots Ken' (Ken Morrison was the Bradford-born chairman). It became very difficult for the company to sell the store, and after a few years all the pressure we put on the company bore fruit. The store was finally spruced up, and rumours abounded that senior management had changed their decision. On 4 May 2010 Morrisons announced it was committed to keeping the store open. Management argued that 'market conditions had changed' but staff later told us that it was the campaign that had saved the store. We had moved a mountain.

Radical alternatives, squatting and sharing

Poverty has many faces in Britain. Those on lower incomes often live with long-term financial hardship, crippling debts, poor housing and education. They have shorter lives than those with higher incomes and are more prone to illness. One of the biggest disadvantages poor people face is the availability of low-cost accommodation. The cost of housing has soared, and for young people starting out, the situation is dire. Those who have to leave the family home, or have moved to another area to look for work, face a particularly difficult time. I remember facing a similar problem when finishing full-time education. A group of us who were active in campaigning wanted to live together, and wanted to challenge the way society organized housing. We came across the work of Radical Roots, a co-operative that gave loans to workers and housing co-operatives, and we began a two-year process of raising funds and looking for the right property. Eventually the Hive Housing co-op was born, and a community of seven anarchists, communists and one liberation theologian got stuck into building a home of activism and solidarity. Our house became a centre for environmental campaigning as well as hosting the city's Local Exchange and Trade Scheme (LETS). LETS encouraged people to barter their skills from plumbing to babysitting based on a non-monetary system. Points, in our case 'Brads', were built up and could be exchanged for anything from guitar lessons to time on a car-share scheme.

The rise in house prices has made it harder for people to set up housing co-ops, but many still try to experiment with co-operative styles of living. In Bradford there are quite a number of squats, some of which are highly elaborate, with electricity and plumbing, with activities to promote more 'politicized' squat living. Young people are tired of seeing properties left empty for decades while they are homeless.

Instead of demonizing squat communities, it is important to try to understand them, and give them as much support as possible. This is not always easy or comfortable. For a while squatters moved into our garage at Desmond Tutu House, so we worked with them to run a free bike repair centre while they stayed there. They eventually moved into a better squat in a neighbouring street. The house had sat empty for many years, having been sold off by the university to a developer. One evening, a group of men turned up with baseball bats, and beat up several of the squatters. Despite the threats, the squatters decided to stay: some were migrant workers from Eastern Europe, and had nowhere else to go. The police eventually evicted them by force and they were dispersed around the city, including a property owned by the cathedral.

The 'Branches Co-operative' is a more sustainable model for Bradford. They set themselves up in a private rented house, living as communally as possible. Many of the Branches people volunteered at the Treehouse Café attached to Desmond Tutu House, and were involved in the Bradford samba band and direct action networks. Jen, a young activist from Branches, organized a food co-op to allow people to buy cheap vegan and organic produce. Others, such as Andrew Dey, threw themselves into working with asylum-seekers and became a valued member of SoulSpace, providing a crucial link to local activist movements.

These experiments in communal living and sharing limited resources provide a small-scale template for how poverty could be tackled in the UK. Churches could use their resources to encourage such activities, and in the process would connect with extremely creative and imaginative young people in their vicinity.

Issue linkage – local and global poverty

Churches do not have to make a choice between working on issues of international poverty or local poverty. If you start addressing poverty close to home you inevitably get a sense of how poverty works itself out at an international level. When you see the impact of privatization on poor communities in England, you realize the impact of privatization on the poorest in the global South. As churches begin to struggle against the cutbacks in local services, we get a sense of the global impact of cuts to the public sector imposed by the IMF and the World Bank. It was reflecting on the impact of poverty on women on the estate I grew up on that made me think deeply about how poverty disproportionately affects women worldwide.

One way of making those links is by supporting the fair trade movement. At Desmond Tutu House we provide a base for fair trade initiatives such as the Treehouse Café and 'Fairgrounds', run by Nina Carter-Brown. The latter is a social enterprise that organizes stalls at festivals such as Greenbelt and Glastonbury, selling fairly-traded goods. It also goes into schools and churches to educate groups about the wider problems of international trade. By supporting fledgling social enterprises such as Fairgrounds, our churches can create a growing awareness of the connections between Western spending behaviour and its impact on some of the world's poorest communities. Fair trade is one springboard to encourage us all to examine the unfair terms of trade that poorer nations face. But the first thing we have to do is tackle problems of greed and income distribution right here. The growing gap between the rich and the poor is orchestrated by the richest nations. We have to challenge the mass inequalities at home if we want to stand side by side with those doing the same throughout the world.

'Listen then if you have ears!': Commitment to make poverty history

Educate

- Invite speakers to your church from groups such as Christian Aid, CAFOD, World Development Movement or War On Want.
- Watch films that look at the impact of multinationals and international organizations such as the IMF. *The Corporation* and Naomi Klein's *The Shock Doctrine* are good places to start.
- Send for resources from development organizations such as OXFAM or the Fairtrade Foundation; make sure that the information is shared and discussed at a church meeting.

Action

- Ensure that your community gets involved in Fairtrade Fortnight or other events such as international 'No Shopping Day' so that people's consumer habits can be explored.
- Get active during Christian Aid Week or other such events when lots of good resources are at hand. Often anti-poverty groups such as Church Action on Poverty or CAFOD have excellent material during Lent and Advent. Christian Aid and USPG usually have excellent harvest time resources to help get your church active in the real issues of poverty and hunger.
- Hold a 'poverty hearing' to tell the stories of those facing poverty in your area.

Reflection

- Regularly hold special services that concentrate on the issues affecting the poorest people of the world. The World Council of Churches and the Iona Community offer some exemplary worship resources on the subject.
- Have a community meeting where you look at the story of Dives and Lazarus, and other teachings on poverty in the Bible. Do you feel motivated and empowered to help create a more equal society? What are the obstacles? What does Jesus have to say about wealth and poverty?
- Use the JustChurch materials offered by Church Action on Poverty to help your group consider how it deals with issues of poverty.
- Read books by theologians such as Barbara Glasson, Ann Morisy, Kathy Galloway and Desmond Tutu. What are these voices saying to our churches?

Sustaining

- Ensure that you subscribe to Christian and campaigning organizations that are tackling the root causes of poverty. Make sure that materials from the Sojourners movement, Christian Aid, Tearfund, CAFOD, USPG are put in a place where your community members and visitors might actually read them.
- Try to see if there are direct links you can make to people living with the effects of poverty.
- Volunteer with organizations working with the homeless, refugees, or those who are in debt.

Chapter 11

Civil Liberties

In order to be part of a prophetic ministry of liberation, we may find ourselves brushing against the law. This can be alarming for Christians, but part of the agenda for liberation theologians today must include defending the right to protest. This right is under threat even in Western liberal societies, as illustrated recently by the powerful documentary *Taking Liberties*. Our church in Bradford has had reason to be concerned about the erosion of civil liberties.

The curious case of Menwith Hill

On 4 July 2008 I found two PCSOs standing outside Desmond Tutu House. We were about to head off to an annual 'Independence from America day' protest up at Menwith Hill, the largest US spybase in the world. It is usually a fun event, often attended by comedians such as Mark Thomas, Jeremy Hardy and Mark Steel. I expected a large police presence at the demonstration but did not expect officers to be posted outside my home. The events of the previous few weeks had been odd indeed. There had been a hunger strike in the Czech Republic as activists highlighted the US 'missile defence system' to be placed on their soil. The Czech peace campaigners had invited people around the world to demonstrate acts of solidarity. The Yorkshire and Humberside branch of the Campaign for Nuclear Disarmament, now based in Desmond Tutu House, wanted to show some support. Sarah Cartin, the CND co-ordinator, popped her head round the door and asked if we wanted to join in the solidarity action. I sent out an email to our church mailing list to see if anyone wanted to take part in a fast outside the gates of Menwith Hill that coming Sunday.

Menwith is situated a few miles west of Harrogate, about 30 miles from Bradford, and we had occasionally joined the evening vigils organized by the Campaign for Accountability of American Bases. Another wayward priest, Ray Gaston, and I had been arrested there on the first anniversary of the outbreak of war in Iraq.

A few days after the email was sent, Sarah received an unusual phone call in the CND office. It was Joe McKenzie, the head of security at Menwith Hill. He often rang up prior to demonstrations to try to assess the scale of the protest. Sarah was surprised when he said that he thought 'Chris and his church' were planning to go to the base that Sunday. Sarah wondered how he could have known that. CND emails were regularly intercepted by the intelligence services, but she had not written anything about our involvement. She came to my office, and asked if I had put anything on our website about it. We had not, which meant that Menwith Hill had been reading our church emails. She gave me Mr McKenzie's contact number and I rang him immediately. He seemed very flustered when I quizzed him about reading our emails. 'A colleague passed me the information, but I think he read it on a website or something,' he explained. 'What is your colleague's name?' I requested, 'can I speak to him?' 'Sorry, I can't give you his name, but I can talk to him when he gets back to work.' 'Is he not there now?' 'No he has . . .' there was a pause; 'gone home for the day to wait for a fridge to be delivered.' This was the head of security at Menwith Hill spybase, and that was the best line he could come up with. 'Could you ring me as soon as you have contacted him?' I persisted; 'I want to know how you came by this information.' He didn't ring back in the next few days, or answer my calls. So I sent an email to our church mailing list. Subject heading: 'Joe McKenzie from Menwith Hill is illegally reading our church emails.' Within a few hours I received a surprising phone call. 'I want an apology,' demanded Mr McKenzie. 'We do nothing illegal on this base and you should apologise for accusing us of doing so.' 'But you are clearly reading our church emails!' I responded. 'Yes, but it is perfectly legal, your emails are available as "open source material".' I didn't know what that meant, but I was not going to apologize: 'Look, legal or not, I don't know; I do know that it's immoral. We have nothing to hide at our church, and I'll happily send you our emails directly, but only if you start coming to services, it might do you some good!'

I thought it was the end of the matter until I saw the two PCSOs standing in the shade of our ash tree an hour before we were to travel up to Menwith. I asked the officers why they were there. 'We are just making use of the shade on this hot day,' one of them replied. I brought out some refreshments and a heavily pregnant Sarah Cartin. 'Are you supposed to spy on us before we get to Menwith Hill?' she said, giving a hard stare toward the officers. 'What's Menwith Hill?' one of the officers retorted. The other officer looked uncomfortable, he knew me from the city-centre Street Angel patrols. 'We are here to check on the numbers going up to the demonstration, and to see which vehicles you are using. It seems a little ridiculous; it's certainly not what I signed up to do.' 'This is a perfectly legal demonstration and this is harassment and intimidation' Sarah stated. 'Who should we complain to?' The officer informed us that, at the earlier briefing, they were told the surveillance order came from North Yorkshire police, and he suggested we should write to them first. We did, and subsequent and drawn-out correspondence produced denials that the orders came from either North or West Yorkshire police services, indicating that it was in fact Menwith Hill that had initiated the operation.

I was happy to tell the officers everything, as we had nothing to hide: 'OK, there are sixteen of us, and we are going up in a bright-pink minibus.' 'A pink minibus?' the first officer scoffed, 'a man of the cloth should know better than to tell lies!' Suddenly the pink minibus drove up. We had failed to organize transport properly, and had ended up with only one option, a bright pink hen-night minibus. The female driver was quizzed by the officers and had to show ID. 'I thought this was supposed to be a free country,' the driver said as we headed off. 'Tell you what, have a party bag each!'

The whole affair left me with a bad taste in my mouth. I was appalled that a US spybase could order local PCSOs to stand outside a church building for over an hour. I received another shock when I mentioned this to a friendly local police support officer. He admitted that they were often asked to watch Desmond Tutu House prior to national and local demonstrations, but most of the officers ignored the order because they knew we were always peaceful.

Christians who go beyond letter-writing and are prepared to stand up to aggressive government policies have always faced overt or covert resistance from the state. Compared to twenty years ago, though, there appear to be far fewer activists prepared to be involved in direct action. It is a long time since Rowan Williams was arrested after protesting at Lakenheath US air base, and I wonder why so few Christians are now involved in prophetic direct action. Part of the reason might be the increasing criminalization of activism. Two members of our church, Lavinia Crossley and Tansy Newman-Turner, suddenly found themselves being charged with legislation passed under the Serious Organized Crime and Police Act (SOCPA) after being involved with a protest. For going over the fence of a military base they would previously have only been charged with the lesser offence of trespass, but under the new SOCPA laws they risked a custodial sentence. Fortunately for the two peace studies graduates, the most serious charges were eventually dismissed by the judge.

Not only have the activities of peace and environmental groups been criminalized, but legitimate protest has been demonized in the press. Activists involved in groups such as Climate Camp and Plane Stupid are often either ridiculed in the media, or their activities are heralded as extremist and violent. This is anything but the truth, as these movements are organized around methods of non-violence. The terrible events of 11 September 2001 and the London bombings of 2005 certainly make an understandable case for increased surveillance of suspected terrorists, but environmental and peace protesters are not terrorists, nor are thousands of young Muslims who feel harassed and intimidated by the surveillance culture of the so-called 'prevent' agenda. The government and the police need to reassess their strategies for dealing with legitimate protest. Christians in turn need to be prepared to put their bodies where their faith leads them.

'The price of freedom is eternal vigilance'

The atrium at the University of Bradford provides a focal point for student life, with a print-shop, a canteen, a café and lots of space in which to generally socialize. The Amnesty International Society decided to do a short piece of drama highlighting capital punishment. Twenty people stood in a circle, and slowly and silently, one by one, dropped to the floor to indicate the number of people executed each day somewhere in the world. Leaflets were to be handed out to passers-by to explain the action. Within a few minutes of the drama commencing, several university security men came over and demanded that the students leave the building. The staff also asked that they hand over their union ID cards. The students decided to leave and finish the drama in the space outside the library. Within a few minutes, two PCSOs arrived and told them that if they continued, they were at risk of being charged with breach of the peace. The students finished their performance in the student union bar, shocked at the University's reaction.

These are minor issues compared to real human-rights abuses in many parts of the world, but it is important that churches safeguard the rights of those who speak out against injustice and invite them into our communities. Christianity should be a home for dissidents, freedom fighters, revolutionaries, poets and prophets. We should be a church of the 'upper room', a place of sharing and symbolic action, preparing ourselves for the confrontation with the powers that be. Imagine if our Eucharistic celebrations were truly a radical memory of the Last Supper. That in the breaking of the bread and the drinking of the wine, we remembered Christ's preparation to have his own body broken, his own blood spilt for God's kingdom of non-violent love. Christians have felt the presence of this radical Jesus strongly over the centuries. It has produced movements for equality, from the Diggers in the seventeenth century to those fighting for black civil rights in the twentieth century. We need to reawaken our radical Christian faith and be bold in building up God's reign of justice and love.

Supporting Amnesty International

One small act which every church can do easily is to spend a short period each week or each month supporting the work of Amnesty International. It is a small thing to write a few words down to protect the life of someone in danger. Faced with an angry male mob determined to wreak vengeance on a female victim, Jesus responded with a simple act of non-violent resistance; he stilled the baying crowd with some markings on the floor. Perhaps he wrote down one of the Ten Commandments: 'Thou shalt not kill'. Writing can save lives.

The work of JustChurch began by regularly writing for Amnesty International as part of our community life. We want to defend the rights of those who face persecution because of their beliefs. Churches can lead people from apathy to activism, and we can start with the small step of writing a letter.

'Listen then if you have ears!': Commitment to civil liberties

Education
- Organize a presentation on civil liberty campaigns.
- Send for information from Liberty, Amnesty International and Human Rights Watch.
- Watch the film *Taking Liberties* and organize a discussion on the issues it presents.

Action
- Organize a letter-writing session for Amnesty International.
- Train to be a legal observer at protests and demonstrations.

Reflection
- Think about the human rights abuses under Roman occupation of Israel; how did Jesus respond? Is there a biblical response to civil liberties?
- Pray about those who have lost their rights because of their religious or political beliefs.

Sustaining
- Make sure that letter-writing for Amnesty International or other such campaigning is a regular part of the life of your church.

Chapter 12

Liberating Conclusions

The emerging church movement will only be a sign of God's love and mercy when it embraces the social justice agenda. We must demonstrate that God is on the side of the earth and its people, and prove the relevance of the gospel in today's society. Jesus came to liberate, and that is the continuing task of twenty-first-century Christians. I hope that this book goes some way to illustrate that liberation theology is alive and well and has much to offer the modern Church.

Protest as mission

The Church must be a visible presence within movements to build a fairer and more just society. When people oppose war, environmental degradation and economic inequalities, Christians need to be at the heart of these movements. Whenever we protest, we make visible God's desire for a better world.

As well as supporting progressive movements, we have a role in instigating protest, becoming agitators for peace. Fresh expressions of Church will find this easier than traditional Church, and can respond to developing situations far more quickly. In this way, new forms of Church may also help the mainstream institutions find a renewed vision for the world. Mission as protest will involve:

- Being at the heart of struggles against climate change and ecological destruction.
- Resisting cutbacks in education, health, social welfare; services that are the backbone of a just society.

- Building alternative models of living that promote equality, sharing and sustainability.
- Working for peace and reconciliation and opposing all that creates conflict and war.
- Involvement in local campaigns to create just communities.
- Being active in international movements to end poverty.
- Taking human rights seriously.
- Participating in movements of solidarity with oppressed communities and nations who are building just societies.

Prophetic ministry

Encouraging the emerging church movements to be active in the social justice agenda is not without its risks, and pioneer and fresh expression ministers will need much support if they are to take these matters seriously. Prophetic ministry is dangerous, but it is part of our faith heritage. Mainstream churches must be risk-takers in funding this kind of ministry. Theological courses need to train ministers who are able to:

- Work with participatory models of church, using dialogical methods to build up the people of God.
- Reach out to other faiths, building bridges of respect and understanding.
- Better understand the inclusive nature of God so that they may challenge inequalities based on race, gender, class, sexual orientation and disability.
- Raise their voices against injustices both local and global, and work collaboratively with those who are building 'another possible world'.
- Be critical of when the Church has got things wrong, and recognize why those outside the Church may have got things right.
- Use the tools of liberation theology to better understand the Bible and God's mission to the world.

Jesus as dissident

The emerging churches need to remember that their focus is on following the will of God. For us as Christians, that means following the rules set out in the Old Testament of Sabbath economics (good stewardship of God's earth) and prophetic justice (redistributing wealth and defending the vulnerable against oppression). It also means rediscovering Jesus as a radical dissident who defied an empire in pursuit of truth and mercy. As Christians we believe that we learn about God's will through the activities and teachings of Jesus. Jesus is a model for discipleship, and we must strive to understand the context of his life and ministry so that we are able to relate them to our own. This will mean:

- Reading the Bible carefully with commentaries that reveal the context of his life and teaching.
- Recognizing the anti-imperial story that is lived out in the Gospel narratives.
- Relating Jesus' dissident discipleship to our own times and our twenty-first-century oppressions.
- Creating new ways of living out our commitment to being peacemakers and justice seekers.
- Resisting the logic of materialism, individualism and consumerism.
- Demonstrating God's love with acts of compassion that build up the common good.

Building the kingdom

Practical liberation theology in the twenty-first century will involve finding new ways of expressing the reign of God. We need to educate faith communities about the realities of sin and oppression, and then have the courage to act in ways that build up a society based on God's vision for earth and humanity. We need to reflect thoughtfully about our actions, constantly bringing our discipleship to God in prayer and thought. We need to use the tools of contemplation to allow the Holy Spirit to move us and guide us. We need to find ways of sustaining ourselves and our movements when we feel overwhelmed by the immensity of the task before us. Building the reign of God will involve:

- Creating communities of faith based on respect and acceptance.
- Becoming more attuned to creation, learning to grow things and desiring to protect nature.
- Noticing injustice when it occurs, and working with others to challenge it.
- Building up solidarity with marginalized communities, locally and internationally.
- Welcoming the stranger and building a culture of hospitality, especially towards those in need of sanctuary.
- Worship that is inclusive and encourages our faith to connect with the outside world.
- Working to eradicate poverty and inequality.
- Seeking practical ways of reconciliation and peace in places of conflict, both locally and globally.
- Finding 'still' places where we can reflect and remember that we are created in the image of God.

We cannot be over-sentimental about the task that we are committed to. A just Church is a difficult and potentially dangerous Church. However, our faith points us in this direction. In the struggle to build this reign of God, a place of love, mercy and hope, we are sustained by the gentle nourishment of the Holy Spirit, and the hope found in Christ. A counter-cultural life will be constantly challenged by those with power, both inside and outside the Church. But we are not alone on this journey. We are joined by the One who overcomes pain and persecution; the One who cannot be nailed to the cross for ever; the One who desires our eternal liberation. If we still ourselves long enough to encounter the one who journeys with us, we will find the strength to build a just Church.

Postscript

Bradford: A Model of Peaceful Resistance to Fascism and Extremism

When the English Defence League (EDL) announced in early 2010 that they were going to hold a static demonstration in Bradford on 28 August, many in the city feared a return to the problems sparked nearly a decade earlier. In 2001 the far right tried to organize a march in the city centre, and though it had been banned, a tiny number of National Front members had managed to stir a riot that had deeply affected the economy and reputation of the city. Everyone in the city began to prepare to make sure that didn't happen again, but nobody believed that it would be easy.

The EDL prepared the ground in May by arriving unannounced during an event to give the freedom of the city to the Yorkshire Regiment. They gathered in a city-centre pub and then 150 of them marched behind the army as the Regiment toured the streets. It was a frightening spectacle. I went into the pub to try and get a sense of who they were and what they really wanted. Many told me they were ex-Army, and wanted to continue the fight against extremism. Most told how Bradford was being taken over and that the Muslims must be defeated. Some told me that we needed to regain England for the white people. Their casual racism then became more evidently disturbing as they processed through the town with aggressive chanting, accompanied by an almost animal-like 'pack' mentality. I revealed a t-shirt that said, 'Fight Poverty not War' and was soon snarled at by EDL supporters. A group of them told me to get out of town, and I had to make a hasty retreat.

That encounter with them led me to open the doors of Desmond Tutu House to the local Unite Against Fascism group (UAF), comprising union activists, local Muslims, students and members of socialist and anti-fascist groups. It was clear that people would come to oppose the EDL gathering in August, and it was important to all of us from the beginning that Bradford's resistance to fascism must be led by the community, and be a peaceful celebration of multiculturalism. We decided to call the event 'WE ARE BRADFORD'.

A few weeks later, another anti-fascist group, 'Hope Not Hate', announced an initiative called 'Bradford Together' which focused on securing a ban on the EDL having a march. Even though this would not stop the EDL gathering for a static demonstration, it would show the city's distaste for the far right. Despite attempts from the 'We are Bradford' group to secure a combined campaign against the EDL, the 'Hope not Hate' grouping constantly attacked the UAF activity, arguing that they were trying to organize violent protest. On top of all this, a week before the EDL's demonstration, the council announced that they would support a group of local community activists who were organizing a second 'celebration' of diversity on a site outside the city centre.

It felt like a real mess, and people were beginning to fall out with each other.

The question for us as a church was, what was our role in all this drama? The answer at Desmond Tutu House was to try to support all who were clearly working for non-violence in the city, and to provide information to our members about what was going on, and allow them to choose how they might best work for peace on that day.

Prayer was our first port of call, and a few days before the big day some of us met at Desmond Tutu House and walked and prayed our way through all the places affected by the EDL gathering. We prayed for peace for the police and council workers at 'Jacob's Well', where 'Bradford Together' were to hold the vigil on the Friday. At Crown Court Plaza, where the 'We are Bradford' celebration was to take place, we prayed for the local and national anti-fascist movements. Then we went down to the Bradford Urban Garden (the Westfield site) where the EDL would be contained. Surrounded by the wild flowers, we prayed for all who get caught up in extremism. Then we prayed for the Cathedral, which had agreed to be a place of sanctuary and prayer on the day, then onwards to Ivegate, where the

'Women for Peace' would be gathering on the Friday. We then prayed for the city hall and the Centenary Square, already fenced off with a huge display saying 'Bradford Peaceful Together'. On the way past the university, we remembered the work of the 'Programme for a Peaceful City' and the work they had done to train community and youth workers in being resilient and keeping the lines of communication open.

There was a lot of fear and anxiety, but after all the prayers I was convinced that God would be able to use the diverse talents of the city to work wonders on the day. I was also determined that those who were trying to divide the opposition to the EDL should not leave a legacy of mistrust between the differing positions on how to oppose the far right. All strategies were valid in their own way: petitioning against the march; ignoring the EDL; diverting young people away from potential conflict; bringing women's voices in; building community resilience; supporting the police; holding cultural events on infirmary fields; holding city-centre events that celebrated multiculturalism and overtly opposed the EDL.

We worked hard with the local and national UAF, and were rewarded by their determination to keep their opposition to the EDL as peaceful as possible. Their training for stewards was exceptional, and went through all the things that could go wrong, and always proposed non-violent reactions to provocation. 'We are Bradford' also tried to encourage local debates to create a public response to the situation. Unfortunately, a large public debate held in Girlington early in August was marred by an extreme left-wing group called 'Workers' Power' who constantly attacked the police despite repeated calls from the speakers at the front to avoid confrontational posturing. Police tactics at previous anti-fascist events had caused understandable concern. The police officers we had invited remained calm and helpful, a sign that they had learnt lessons from the past, and were determined that the Bradford situation would be very different.

I also tried to support those in the community who decided at the last minute to hold a 'mela' type event at Infirmary Fields, just outside the city centre. I wished that we had held a joint event, but recognized why they felt that they couldn't work alongside the 'We are Bradford' celebration. Some were fearful of encouraging families into the city centre on that day, and some had believed council officers and 'Hope not Hate' activists who said that the UAF were out to cause a riot. Some genuinely believed that the reaction to the EDL must only involve local people and not work with those nationally opposed to the rise of the far right.

Our church promoted the amazing work of the 'Bradford Women for Peace' network, who paved the way for non-violence with a series of imaginative stunts including a human web of interconnectedness held the day before the EDL arrived. Lime-green ribbon joined together hundreds of women from all faiths and none in a sign of solidarity. The ribbons were spread thoughout the city, and a giant ribbon even draped the Cathedral entrance. The women of Bradford led the way again.

The churches supported the 'Hope Not Hate' peace vigil the night before, joining the singing of 'We shall overcome' with council workers and faith leaders. David Ison, the Dean of the Cathedral, spoke eloquently, and a tree of peace was adorned with written prayers and thoughts.

The big day came, and in the morning we prepared ourselves with prayers at the Cathedral. Many church leaders were there, and the gathering was hugely important as we felt God's hand on us for the difficult hours to come. I accompanied Barbara Glasson, David Ison, Helen Tanner, Sam Jackson, Clare Maclaren and Ernest Lennon into the city centre, heading past the urban gardens where the EDL supporters were beginning to muster. Small groups of white lads angrily marched by, covering their faces, gathering people and speeding round the city centre. Church ministers went to various parts of the city, hoping to help keep things calm. We kept thanking Muslim community leaders who were doing the same thing. Everything was looking hopeful. I was just about to speak at the 'We are Bradford' event when Barbara Glasson, my Methodist colleague, rang to say that the EDL had begun to hurl missiles and smoke bombs. We all agreed on the stage to keep everyone calm and safely in the Square. It was hugely important that people did not all rush down to see what was happening, and we stuck to the celebratory feel of the day. In my speech I thanked the local people who had gathered and those from far and wide who had come to show their solidarity with the people of Bradford, I then discreetly headed off to make sure Barbara was all right. The situation at the urban gardens was tense. Bricks had been hurled from the EDL demonstration, aimed at the young Muslims who had come to make sure that the EDL stayed where they were and didn't come any further into the city. Barbara had been doing a fantastic job talking to the people and simply being lovely and calm. I handed out sweets to those who were not fasting during Ramadan. Suddenly there were more surges, as members of the EDL tried to push through the police lines. The police did an amazing job keeping them back. Several hundred EDL supporters then tried to escape over the walls, and for a moment the situation looked grim. The Cathedral staff had to lock themselves in. Rumours were out that EDL members wanted to attack a mosque in Manningham. I relayed what was happening to my contacts in the 'operations room' of the police and council and followed the hundreds of mostly Asian youths who headed off to stop the EDL members getting into the Manningham area. There was a small pitched battle, and the EDL supporters soon ran back to the police lines and were eventually herded into coaches waiting to take them out of Bradford.

The EDL was crushed. They had predicted a turnout of up to 10,000, but only managed possibly 800. They had claimed to be non-racist, but they were exposed by the chants they sang and the placards they displayed. They claimed to be peaceful, but they had brought weapons, bricks and smoke bombs.

More importantly, the riots they had hoped to provoke never materialized. There were a handful of arrests, mostly of EDL members. The police had shown restraint, local communities showed determination and calmness, and thousands of local people were involved in making sure that the difficulties of the past were not relived. Bradford had shown itself to be a city of peace even in a situation of extreme stress.

My hope is that despite the tangle of positions and the complexity of relations in the city, we can show that Bradford is well on the way to recovering its reputation and can demonstrate its commitment to the politics and theology of hope, respect and non-violence.

God is in the most difficult of places, and our mission is to be in the midst of them also, witnessing to a God of peace who demonstrates real hope for humanity and creation. From opposing fascism to challenging inequalities, liberation theology offers an important tool for dealing with the new challenges of the twenty-first century.

Afterword

This is a joyful book. It is a book about liberation and the way in which faith can liberate the human spirit. But it is also a deeply challenging book, an account of what can happen when we take faith out and about with us, when we let it seep into our souls and bring a thirst for justice. It is at times an unsettling read, and for that I praise God: the unsettling of our assumptions and comfortable lives is a sign of the Spirit at work, moving us to action and engagements within and beyond our communities.

We can probably all tell stories of liberation when we look back. Looking forward is much harder work – we are all faced with the massive challenges of our lives and situations, and issues most often descend upon us in confusion and chaos. Reading Chris's account of JustChurch and SoulSpace may cause us to think that protest ministry is a clear-cut process, a succession of wonderful and committed people and issues that presented themselves to him in some sort of logical order. This is not the case; I know this because since my arrival in Bradford, Chris and I have walked and talked our way around the city. And in the light of the recent murder of three street workers, we have prayed our way around too.

What is remarkable in Chris's writing is that he is able to relate the daily dilemmas and challenges that have faced him in Bradford and beyond and continually make the connection between his experience and Christian gospel in practical and engaging ways. This is because he is passionate both about his faith and the place where he lives. He is simply prepared to put his body where his beliefs are. He lives what he speaks, and this is incarnation.

What is unusual about SoulSpace and JustChurch is that they do not fit into the conventional expectations of 'fresh expressions'. They are not simply 'old church with doughnuts' but have an undergirding theology of liberation which informs their prayer and protest. They remind us that the work of the Church is not to fill its pews but to change the world, bring good news to the poor and set oppressed people free. If people are inspired through such action to come to church, then all well and good, but it is not the reason for the Church existing. Through such fresh insights and engagement it is highly likely that the Church will be transformed into a new way of being. This is both wonderful and scary. The spirit of God is not about safety but a movement to act on behalf of the world.

Witnessing to the stories and concerns of Bradford is a costly as well as an empowering story. When the Church's mission strategies engage with 'fresh expressions' we rarely discuss any cost that isn't financial. The cost of the Kingdom, as embodied by Chris and his companions, is far more radical than balancing the books. It is a cost of vulnerability through solidarity with those who are disempowered both at home and in the wider world. It is a cost in shoe leather, time and attention as well as personal security. It is about being vulnerable to whatever the day brings, and it is an exercise in resilience and sometimes sheer bloody-mindedness. It is an investment in the lives of individuals as well as in politics and economics. This sort of investment is a long-term project: places like Bradford require Christian people to 'hang on in there' and embody the commitment of Christ to people for whom life is often too hard.

Will the inherited, traditional Church be able to sustain the long-term project that emerges from 'fresh expression' initiatives? Will it be able to honour the commitment of priests and people who have lived in solidarity with the poorest and continue to enable a theology of liberation to be enacted in our place? I think the jury is still out. Traditional structures want to take risks until they are successful; the second part, the part when the initial groundbreaking work needs to be undergirded and stabilized, that's where the courage of the institution can begin to waver. That's where conversations about finance so often quell the flames of the new life that is being born. It will be interesting to see how this is worked out at Desmond Tutu House.

'Fresh expressions' is not a quick fix for the Church, it is an attempt to move afresh with the wind of the Spirit that blows where it will. For people like Chris, and those at SoulSpace and JustChurch, this means taking risks that bring them both to the edge of the law and their communities. It is these risks that make sense of the gospel and enable people with radical understanding to comprehend that faith is not something ethereal and remote. Through this engagement with radical theology, the things of God begin to make sense. People become inspired to change the world for the sake of justice and peace.

JustChurch and SoulSpace make faith seem possible. They inspire people to belong to a community that can be honest and open. They engage with reality and look for practical strategies to change the world. The role of the priest is to continually reflect theologically on what this means and how the stories of God can be heard. It is demanding work alongside a fluid community, and requires both wit and wisdom to sustain. Chris Howson has both of these, and a deep commitment to Bradford too. Alongside Chris, my hope is that we Methodists can develop a 'listening community' that can help support this work with safe space for quiet reflection, prayer and gentleness. This partnership will offer a new sort of ecumenism in which we can be both friends and deepen the Christian conversation. This is so important in a city that is predominantly Muslim and in which interfaith dialogue is about how we relate creatively and honestly with our Asian neighbours. Churches working together in supportive partnership is a sign of hope in challenging circumstances, a witness to the importance of faith to our city and beyond.

Bradford doesn't always feel as though it is leading the way in the world, but through the work that is happening through Chris and Desmond Tutu House, it can demonstrate how a small enterprise of faith can begin to lead the way – how 'protest' can be a movement towards empowerment of the voiceless. This is a good book, and once you have read it, I hope you will ask, 'Now what can I engage with in my place that will change the world?'

Barbara Glasson

Bibliography

Aguilar, M. (2007), *The History and Politics of Latin American Theology, Vol. 1*. London: SCM Press.

Allen, J. (2006), *Rabble-rouser for Peace: The Authorised Biography of Desmond Tutu*. London: Rider Books.

Allen, O. W. Jr (2005), *The Homiletic of All Believers*. Louiseville, KY: Westminster John Knox Press.

Althaus-Reid, M., Petrella, I. and Susin, L. C. (2007), *Another Possible World*. London: SCM Press.

Ateek, N. S. (2008), *A Palestinian Cry for Reconciliation*. Maryknoll, NY: Orbis Books.

Boff, C. (1990), *Feet-on-the-ground Theology: A Brazilian Journey*. Maryknoll, NY: Orbis Books.

Boff, L. (1995), *Ecology and Liberation*. Maryknoll, NY: Orbis Books.

Boff, L. and Boff, C. (1987), *Introducing Liberation Theology*. Tunbridge Wells: Burns and Oates.

Bradstock, A. and Rowland, C. (eds) (2002), *Radical Christian Writings: A Reader*. Oxford: Blackwell Publishers Ltd.

Cardenal, E. (1977), *Love in Practice: The Gospel in Solentiname*. London: Search Press Ltd.

Carlsson, C. (2008), *Nowtopia*. Edinburgh: AK Press.

Casaldáliga, P. (1990), *In Pursuit of the Kingdom*. Maryknoll, NY: Orbis Books.

Cassidy, S. (1991), *Good Friday People*. London: Darton, Longman & Todd.

Christo, C. (1978), *Letters from a Prisoner of Conscience*. London: Lutterworth Press.

Cochrane, J. (1999), *Circles of Dignity: Community Wisdom and Theological Reflection*. Minneapolis, MN: Augsburg Fortress.

Dennis, M., Golden, R. and Wright, S. (2000), *Oscar Romero: Reflections on His Life and Writings*. Maryknoll, NY: Orbis Books.

Freire, P. (1972), *Pedagogy of the Oppressed*. Harmondsworth, Middlesex: Penguin Books.

145

Galloway, K. (2008), *Sharing the Blessing: Overcoming Poverty and Working for Justice*. London: SPCK and Christian Aid.

Gaston, R. (2009), *A Heart Broken Open*. Glasgow: Wild Goose Publications.

Grassi, J. A. (2006), *Jesus is Shalom: A Vision of Peace From the Gospels*. New York: Paulist Press.

Gutiérrez, G. (1984), *We Drink from Our Own Wells: The Spiritual Journey of a People*. Maryknoll, NY: Orbis Books.

Gutiérrez, G. (1997), *Sharing the Word Through the Liturgical Year*. London: Geoffrey Chapman.

Gutiérrez, G. (2001), *A Theology of Liberation*. London: SCM Press.

Halper, J. (2008), *An Israeli in Palestine*. London: Pluto Press.

Hardy, C. (2007), *Cowboy in Caracas*. Willimantic, KT: Curbstone Press.

Hill, B. (1998), *Christian Faith and the Environment: Making Vital Connections*. Maryknoll, NY: Orbis Books.

Hinton, J. (2002), *Changing Churches*. London: Churches Together in Britain and Ireland.

Horsley, R. A. (2008), *In the Shadow of Empire*. Louiseville, KY: Westminster John Knox Press.

Horsley, R. A. and Silberman, N. A. (1997), *The Message and the Kingdom*. New York: Grosset/Putnam.

Jara, J. (1993), *Victor: An Unfinished Song*. London: Jonathan Cape.

Kember, N. (2007), *Hostage in Iraq*. London: Darton, Longman and Todd.

Kent, D. (1996), *Dorothy Day: Friend to the Forgotten*. Cambridge: William B. Eerdmans Publishing Co.

Klein, N. (2008) *The Shock Doctrine*. London: Penguin Press.

Lees, J. (2007), *Word of Mouth: Using the Remembered Bible for Building Community*. Glasgow: Wild Goose Publications.

López Vigil, J. I. and López Vigil, M. (2000), *Just Jesus*. New York: Crossroad Publishing.

Malina, B. J. and Rohrbaugh, R. L. (1992), *Social Science Commentary on the Synoptic Gospels*. Minneapolis, MN: Fortress Press.

McClure, J. S. (1995), *The Round Table Pulpit*. Nashville: Abingdon Press.

Mesters, C. (1989), *Defenceless Flower: A New Reading of the Bible*. Maryknoll, NY: Orbis Books.

Mesters, C. (1995), *God, Where are You?: Rediscovering the Bible*. Maryknoll, NY: Orbis Books.

Myers, C. (2002), *Binding the Strong Man: A Political Reading of Mark's Story of Jesus*. Maryknoll, NY: Orbis Books.

Petrella, I. (2008), *Beyond Liberation Theology: A Polemic*. London: SCM Press.

Rose, L. (1997), *Sharing the World: Preaching in the Roundtable Church*. Louiseville, KT: Westminster John Knox Press.

Segovia, F. and Sugirtharajab, R. (2009), *A Postcolonial Commentary on the New Testament Writings*. London: T&T Clark.

Shakespeare, S. and Rayment-Pickard, H. (2006), *The Inclusive God*. Norwich: Canterbury Press.

Singh, R. (2002), *The Struggle for Racial Justice*. Bradford: Print Plus UK.

Tutu, D. (1995), *The Rainbow People of God: South Africa's Victory Over Apartheid*. London: Bantam Books.

Wilpert, G. (2003), *Coup Against Chavez in Venezuela*. Caracas, Venezuela: Fundación por un Mundo Multipolar y Fundación Venezolana para la Justicia Global.

Wink, W. (2003), *Jesus and Nonviolence: a Third Way*. Minneapolis, MN: Augsburg Fortress.

Zaru, J. (2008), *Occupied with Nonviolence: A Palestinian Woman Speaks*. Minneapolis, MN: Augsburg Fortress.

Zelter, A. (2001), *Trident on Trial*. Edinburgh: Luath Press.

Zelter, A. (ed.) (2005), *Faslane 365: A Year of Antinuclear Blockades*. Edinburgh: Luath Press.

Helpful Publications, Websites and Filmography

Magazines
Christian Aid News (quarterly) www.christianaid.org.uk
Church Times (weekly) www.churchtimes.co.uk
Cornerstone (quarterly) www.sabeel.org
Cuba Si (quarterly) www.cuba-solidarity.org.uk
Ethical Consumer (bi-monthly) www.ethicalconsumer.org
Morning Star (daily) www.morningstaronline.co.uk
Movement (quarterly) www.movement.org.uk
New Internationalist (monthly) www.newint.org
Red Pepper (bi-monthly) www.redpepper.org.uk
SidebySide (CAFOD) www.cafod.org.uk
Sojourners (monthly) www.sojo.net

Websites
www.amnesty.org.uk
www.babymilkaction.org
www.bradfordsoulspace.org
www.burmacampaign.org
www.caat.org.uk (Campaign Against Arms Trade)
www.chedmyers.org (progressive theologian)
www.christian-ecology.org.uk
www.church-poverty.org.uk
www.climatecamp.org.uk
www.cnduk.org (Campaign for Nuclear Disarmament)
www.ekklesia.co.uk (progressive source of Christian news)
www.fairtrade.org.uk
www.figtree.org.uk (radical non-violence community)
www.foe.org (Friends of the Earth)
www.for.org.uk (Fellowship of Reconciliation)
www.freetibet.org
www.freshexpressions.org.uk
www.inclusivechurch2.net
www.indymedia.org.uk (important source for alternative news)
www.iona.org.uk
www.left-click.net (Venezuela Solidarity Campaign)
www.lgcm.org.uk (Lesbian and Gay Christian Movement)
www.maryknoll.org
www.nosweat.org.uk (campaigning for labour rights)
www.opendemocracy.net
www.palestinecampaign.org

www.progressio.org (development issues)
www.quaker.org
www.speak.org.uk (justice youth movement)
www.stopwar.org.uk
www.tcpc.org (The Centre for Progressive Christianity)
www.tearfund.org
www.tridentploughshares.org (campaign against Trident missiles)
www.utusheffield.org.uk (Urban Theology Unit)
www.waronwant.org
www.wcc-coe.org (World Council of Churches)
www.wdm.org.uk (World Development Movement)

Filmography (films and documentaries that made us think)
Aprile (1997) Moretti, N.
The Age of Stupid (2009) Armstrong, F.
Amandla! (2002) Hirsch, L.
American History X (1999) Kaye, T.
Battle for Haditha (2007) Broomfield, N.
Bowling for Columbine (2002) Moore, M.
Budrus (2010) Bacha, J.
Burma VJ (2009) Østergaard, A.
Capitalism: A Love Story (2009) Moore, M.
Che: Part One (2009) Soderbergh, S.
Children of Men (2006) Cuarón, A.
The Corporation (2005) Bakan, J.
The Crime of Father Amaro (2002) Carrera, C.
Crude: The Real Price of Oil (2009) Berlinger, J.
Cry Freedom (1987) Attenborough, R.
Dr Martin Luther King, Jr (2002) Friedman, T.
The End of the Line (2009) Murray, R.
Garden State (2006) Braff, Z.
The Imam and the Pastor (2006) Channer, A.
Into the Wild (2008) Penn, S.
The Iron Wall (2006) Alatar, M.
Jesus of Montreal (1989) Arcand, B.
Keeping the Faith (2001) Norton, E.
The Lives of Others (2007) Henckel, F.
Machuca (2004) Wood, A.
The Miracle Maker (2000) Hayes, D.
The Mission (1986) Joffé, R.
Mugabe and the White African (2009) Thompson, A. and Bailey, L.
Priest (1995) Bird, A.
Raining Stones (1993) Loach, K.
The Revolution Will Not Be Televised (2003) Bartley, K. and O'Brian, D.
The Shock Doctrine (2010) Whitecross, M & Winterbottom, M.
Son of Man (2007) Dornford-May, M.
Standard Operating Procedure (2008) Morris, E.
Taking Liberties (2007) Atkins, C.
The Truman Show (1998) Weir, P.
Under the Bombs (2007) Aractingi, P.
Wal-Mart: The High Cost of Low Price (2006) Greenwald, R.
The Wave (2009) Gansel, D.
The War on Democracy (2007) Pilger, J.

Acknowledgements

Much of this book was written during a three-month break in Uruguay and I thank Bishop David James and the Diocese of Bradford for allowing me that space to write and to think. My family and I were made welcome in Tacuarembó by Alison, Jess, Bill, Anna and Gabriella. In Montevideo we were grateful for the use of Bishop Miguel Tamayo's house and I thank the Diocese of Uruguay for all their support. The Catholic Diocese of Rivera and Tacuarembó generously allowed me to use the Capilla de Iporá as a place of prayer and reflection.

I would like to thank all those who have come and prayed and shared with me at Desmond Tutu House, all those who have come to SoulSpace and JustChurch and dared to tell their stories. Special thanks to Lubna, Andrew, Nina, Anna, Jen, Lavinia, Rimoaine, Rebecca, Tansy and Ben, James, Helen Mac and Helen Ap, Sarah, Daniel, Welmoed, Maya, Lorna, Clive, Katrina, Chris, Paul, Debbie, David, Graham, Ceri, Martin, Tom, Spencer, Alice, Alicia, Sirin, Paul, Paula, Ivo, Ed, Keith, Christy, Harry, Fred, Moses, Michelle, Akachi, Umuchi, Ulalu, Sensimelia, Nyasha, Jonathan, Wanda, Albert, Eunice, Caran, Tracey, Stacie, Cacey, Alison, Mateusz, Arran, Liz, Esther, Libby, Jemima, Sally, Sophie, Younis, Caroline, Sue, Jill, Adam, Jennifer, Emily, Emma, Nicky, Paulina, Maarja, Lefteris, Chris, Ernest, Mary, CJ, Angeline, Apeles, Sande, Jackson, Jess, Ica, Joe, Tshepiso, Miriam, Sam, Heather, Richard, Hannah, Sugie, Angela, Matthew, Ruth, Matt, Vanessa, Louise, Yvette, Zayon, Becca, Henry, Mel, Van Helsing, Xiao Mei, Karen, Lucy, Mercy, Alisa, Jane, Cat, Helen B., Josh, Eithne, and the many others who have joined us on our spiritual adventures.

Many thanks to all at the Treehouse Café, especially Jen, Katie, Joe, Joel and Sarah. I'm grateful for the support of all at Yorkshire Campaign for Nuclear Disarmament (CND); the dedication of Anna, Sarah, Denise, Dave and Hannah helps remind me that a nuclear-free world is possible.

Campaigning to support those seeking sanctuary would not be possible without Janet, Caren, Mary, Birita and Brian, Ben and Kongosi or the support of Judy Midgley, Geoff Reid, Rita Armitage, and all involved with Bradford Ecumenical Action Concern (BEACON), especially Will Sutcliffe and Laura O'Connor.

Many thanks to those committed to making a difference in Bradford, to Mike and Salma from Bradford Resource Centre; Daniel, Jonny, Jane, Sue, Rupert and other former members of the Hive Housing Co-op; all the new activists emerging from the Branches Housing Co-op; Graham and Sofia and all who have endured my lack of rhythm at samba band practice. Thanks to Barbara Glasson at Touchstone; David Ison; Andy and Jennifer Williams and Frankie Ward at the Cathedral. I have been blessed in campaigning alongside those who work miracles with limited resources, they include Mary Dowson at Bradford Community Broadcasting; Andy Sykes; Joe Batt; Mollie and David Somerville; Heather Grinter; Noa Kleinman from Amnesty International; Jane Skudders of Friends of the Earth; Nasar Fiaz from the Faiths Forum; Nafees Nasir from United 4 Palestine; Karl and Gloria Dallas from Palestine Solidarity Campaign and Lesley McGorrigan, convenor of Bradford's Stop the War Coalition. Thanks also to Brenda and Keith Thompson for all their efforts for peace and equality; John Anderson and his tireless work for global justice and fair trade; for Adam Clarke, John Dinsdale and all the 'Angels' who have walked the streets with me; Claudia Powell and Sofie Shaw of the German Church; David Jackson, Sr Roisin, Sr Mary and all at the Columba Community. Thanks also to Ludi Simpson and Pat Fuller of the Bradford Cuba Solidarity Campaign; William Wagstaff at the New Beehive Inn and all the anarchists who keep the '1 in 12' going. Thanks to Lisa Cummings, Tariq Shabir, Phillip Lewis and all connected to the ICLS programme. I'm grateful to Liz Firth, Ashiq, Paul, Jonathan, Dusty and all opposed to fascism in Bradford. Thanks also to Paddy McGuffin of the *Morning Star* and

152 *Acknowledgements*

those who lived with us at Desmond Tutu House, especially Martin Pearson and Mary Dobbing.

Many have helped me along my spiritual journey, and special guidance has come from Carol Howson, Malcolm King, Patrick Curran, Mike Harrison, Ruth Weston, Marion Watt, Keith Hebden, Ray Gaston, George Moffat, Chris Hughes, Charles Read, Alan Bartlett, Inderjit Bhogal, John Vincent, Ali Saunders and Judy Hirst. Personal support has often come from those outside the church and I am indebted to Ellie and Will, Karen, Claudia and a host of living angels.

A special thank you goes to Alex and Katie Jones who have helped with my ministry in so many ways, and to Gordon, Lis and all the Dey family who have supported my wife and me with continual love and wisdom.

This book would not have happened without Ann Morisy and Caroline Chartres from Continuum for coming up with the original idea, Emma Zvesper and Sally Fildes-Moss who worked hard to tidy up many of my mistakes on the manuscript. The blame lies entirely with them!

The final thanks go to my wife and children. Catriona left her beloved home in Uruguay to put up with me here in Bradford. Her love and endurance, along with the hugs of my beloved girls Clara and Angela, made this book possible.